FIRST FLIGHT

A Beginner's Guide to RC Airplanes: How to Buy the Right Plane and Teach Yourself to Fly!

By Stephen Weber

All Rights Reserved © 2014 by Stephen Weber

No part of this book may be reproduced or transmitted in any form by any means, graphic, electronic, or mechanical, including photocopying, recording, taping or by any information storage or retrieval system, without permission in writing from the publisher.

The information in this book is offered with the understanding that it does not contain legal, financial, or other professional advice. Individuals requiring such services should consult a competent professional. The author and publisher make no representations about the suitability of the information contained in this book for any purpose. This material is provided "as is" without warranty of any kind.

Although every effort has been made to ensure the accuracy of the contents of this book, errors and omissions can occur. The publisher assumes no responsibility for any damages arising from the use of this book, or alleged to have resulted in connection with this book.

This book is not completely comprehensive. Some readers may wish to consult additional books for advice. This book is not authorized or endorsed by any company mentioned in the text.

Published by Stephen W. Weber
Printed in the United States of America
Weber Books   www.WeberBooks.com
ISBN: 978-1-936560-23-3

Contents

- **▶ INTRODUCTION** 5
  - *The Principles of Flight* 8

- **▶ THE FIVE BEST BEGINNER PLANES** 11
  - *Ready-to-Fly vs. Bind-n-fly* 12
  - *HobbyZone Champ* 13
  - *HobbyZone Duet* 14
  - *HobbyZone Sport Cub S with SAFE Technology* 16
  - *UMX Radian* 17
  - *Delta Ray with SAFE Technology* 19
  - RECOMMENDED SECOND PLANES 21
  - *Apprentice 15e with SAFE Technology* 21
  - *Parkzone Radian* 23
  - *Parkzone Sport Cub* 25
  - *ParkZone T-28 Trojan* 26
  - *Great Planes ElectriFly EP Super Sportster* 28
  - *DHC-2 Beaver* 29

- **▶ TEACH YOURSELF TO FLY** 31
  - *Taking Off* 32
  - *Flying Your Plane* 32
  - *Flying in an Oval Pattern* 33
  - *Resisting the Tendency to Overcorrect* 34
  - *Controlling the Plane as It's Flying Toward You* 35
  - *Landing the Airplane* 36
  - *Flaring Your Plane for Touchdown* 37
  - *Don't Fight the Weather* 38

Trimming Your Plane *38*

Hand-launching Your Plane *40*

TROUBLESHOOTING 41

Aircraft Propeller Pulses *41*

Aircraft Control Aurfaces Are Out of Alignment *41*

Aircraft Doesn't Respond to Transmitter Inputs *41*

Aircraft Climbs Too Steeply or Stalls *41*

Throttle Does Not Respond, but Other Controls Work as Expected. *41*

Elevator or Other Surface Oscillates or Flutters During Flight *41*

REPAIRING YOUR AIRCRAFT 42

▶ ACCESSORIES BUYING GUIDE 43

Computer Flight Simulator *43*

Battery Charger *45*

Floats *46*

Cameras *47*

First Person View (FPV) *48*

Smartphone Apps *48*

Lights for Night Flying *49*

▶ JOIN A CLUB 51

AMA Insurance Coverage *54*

Earning the Right to Fly Solo at Your Club Field *54*

▶ FINDING MORE INFORMATION 57

More RC Plane Reviews *58*

Flight Instruction *59*

Recommended Reading *59*

▶ GLOSSARY 61

INDEX 65

▶ INTRODUCTION

The winter when I was 12 years old, I received an exciting present under the Christmas tree: a gas-powered model airplane. When I saw that plane lying beneath the cellophane, my heart started pounding. A plane! Of all the gifts I received that year, nothing held more potential than that shiny new plane. Unfortunately, it was the biggest disappointment.

When it warmed up after Christmas, I walked with Dad across the street to the church parking lot, our neighborhood playground. He rigged up the plane (it was tethered with two strings) and filled it with fuel. After an agonizing wait, while Dad squinted at the instruction manual, he got the engine started. Whirrrr!!!!!! The plane lurched forward, rose a few inches, and banged against the ground. Dad pivoted around in a circle, yanking at the strings, but never got the plane more than a few inches off the ground. Every time it rose a bit, BAM, it would hit the ground again. After half an hour of pure frustration, we packed up the plane and walked home. That plane never came out of its box again. It was too complicated for me, and Dad didn't want to deal with it either.

So much for the "good old days."

Fast-forward 40 years to this past summer. Now I've got a young son of my own. I'm always on the lookout for fun stuff we can do together. And it's not easy to get a kid's attention these days, with competition from TV, video games, tablets, smartphones and computers. But here is one thing that can get kids off the couch: a radio-controlled airplane. After seeing a YouTube video of a flying RC plane, my boy asked for one. I thought about it for a few seconds. Why not? Christmas was still six months away, but we could call it a "late birthday present." I found a plane on Amazon and paid extra for overnight shipping.

It's weird. Every time I get excited about giving someone a gift, it turns out to be something I really wanted for myself.

The next day, the UPS driver left the package—a ready-to-fly Champ RC airplane. Before the school bus brought my son home that day, I was already at the local park, flying that Champ. Well, "flying" is a charitable way of saying that I launched it, and within a few minutes, destroyed it. First I crashed it into the ground. Then I rammed it into a chain link fence. Then I hit the scoreboard at the softball field. And then I got it stuck in a tree, 75 feet above the ground. Pure disaster. And as I walked home, I realized: I was bitten by the RC flying bug. And nothing has been the same since.

Since last summer, I've taken a crash course in RC planes. Literally. And by reading this book, you will benefit from all that mayhem. Most of my mistakes were easily preventable, and I'll tell you how.

The carnage continued after I lost the Champ. Within the next week, I bought two more Champs, and lost them, too. Every time the UPS guy would drop off the next package, my wife would give me a look. "Another plane? What for?!?"

Because I was addicted, that's what for.

Meanwhile, I read every book and magazine article about RC planes I could find. It was frustrating. Everything I found had either way too much information, or way too little. Anything more than a few pages long was horribly out of date. The book you're reading right now is what I wish I could have read last summer. It would have saved me a mountain of angst and a serious slice of my disposable income.

Eventually, I got on track. It's a lot easier to fly RC planes now than it was 40 years ago. There's been a revolution, thanks to the miniaturization and lower cost of tiny electronics and rechargeable batteries. These days you can buy a ready-to-fly plane, charge the battery, and be in the air within an hour. And that's part of the problem. Now it's so easy to get into the air, you can get there long before you're ready.

This book focuses on the newer, easy-to-use "electric" planes, which means that the motor is powered by a battery. The wings and fuselages of these planes are usually made from durable, lightweight Styrofoam. The alternative—internal-combustion planes like the one I got when I was a kid, are still favored by many RC hobbyists. But those planes are generally too noisy, dirty, and complicated for the beginner hobbyist for whom this book is intended.

When I first began working on this book, I hesitated. After all, what qualifications did I have to write a book about flying airplanes, something I'd hardly thought about until six months ago? Simple. It's not rocket science. I'm just helping you avoid the same bone-headed mistakes I made. It all boils down to preparation. And if by spending an hour or two reading this book, you can avoid buying the wrong plane—or avoid a crash or two—it will be worth it.

No matter how smart they are, thousands of people every year jump into the RC plane hobby, and many repeat the same mistakes. The most common mistakes are:

Buying the wrong plane. Lots of folks get into the RC plane hobby by buying a Porsche when they should have bought a Chevy. You've got to buy a plane that matches your skill level – one that can fly slowly until you've learned to control the plane. You need a durable plane that can withstand several hard landings without cracking into pieces. Luckily, many of the inexpensive planes I'll recommend in this book are also the most durable.

Wasting money on the wrong accessories, and not getting the right accessories. New hobbyists face a bewildering array of parts and accessories. For example, do you need extra batteries? What kind of batteries? Do you need a battery charger? Which one? What kind of transmitter do you need? Can you use your existing transmitter with your future planes?

Being impatient. In my first three months in the RC plane hobby, I lost and crashed more than a dozen planes, simply because I wasn't properly prepared and didn't exercise patience—like trying to fly during bad weather. I will show you how to prepare yourself for the best chance at success.

Having no plan for takeoffs, flying, and landing before you leave home. We'll go over the basics of piloting a model plane, and how to do it safely while having fun. Don't wait until you have a plane in the air before you start learning. Start now. I'll give simple instructions on how to take off, fly and land while keeping your risks of accident and injury as low as possible.

Getting Ready

It's true, you can buy a plane and have it in the air within an hour. But before you do that, you should spend some time getting ready. There are three great ways to begin your education, and I recommend that you take advantage of all three, if possible:

1. **Use a computer flight simulator**. For about $100, you can own a realistic training aid that can teach you all the basic tasks of flight. Although flying a model airplane might look

easy, it isn't. In fact, flying an RC plane is in some ways harder to learn than flying a "real" plane. That's because when the plane is flying toward you, you've got to reverse the stick commands – you need to turn "left" to make the plane go right – and so on. Practice on a simulator, and it will be second-nature after a few hours. Buying a simulator can save you hundreds or thousands of dollars in crashes that won't happen. I'll recommend the best simulators in this book.

2. **Get lessons from an experienced hobbyist**. Believe it or not, you can get flying lessons absolutely free at RC clubs across the United States. I urge you to join your local chapter of the Academy of Model Aeronautics, the AMA. More on that later.

3. **Fly at a proper flying field with safety protocols**. Here's the biggest reason to join the AMA—you'll get access to a dedicated flying field. Plus, membership in the AMA includes an insurance policy covering you for liability, medical expenses, fire and theft.

The Principles of Flight

Before we start shopping for planes, let's take a look at what makes an airplane fly. No matter what plane you have, it's subject to the same aerodynamics that the Wright Brothers wrestled with a century ago. The illustration below shows the four forces that affect airplanes:

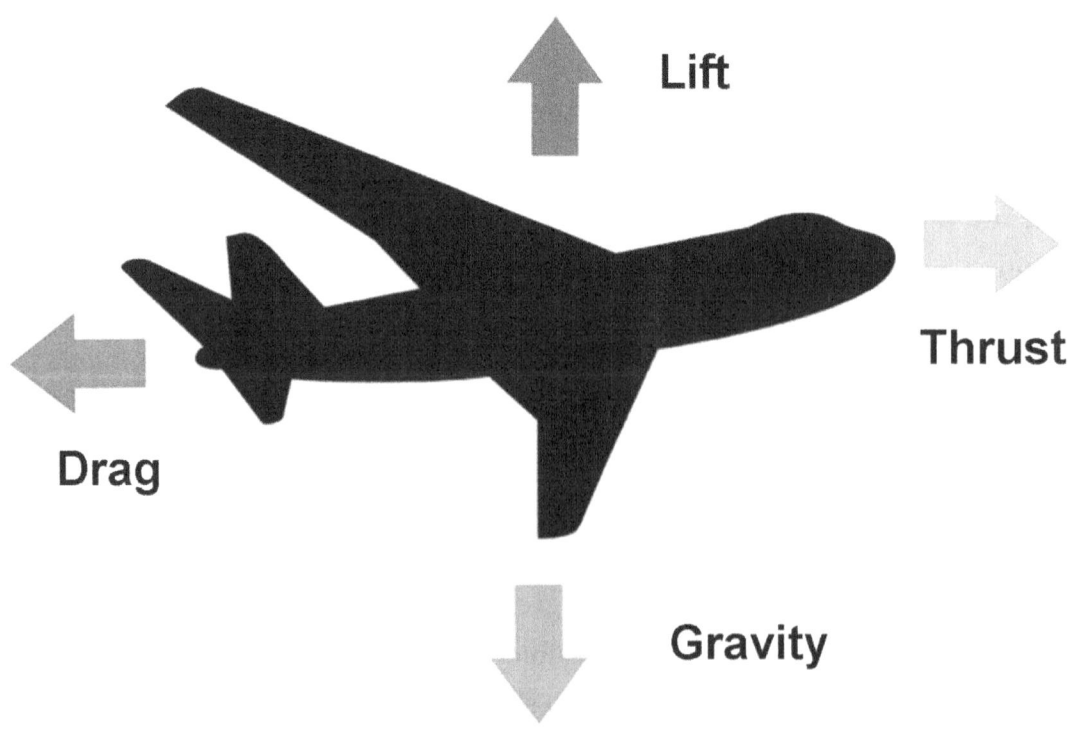

Above: The four forces that affect airplanes.

1. **Gravity** pulls the plane toward the Earth.
2. **Lift** generated by the wing helps raise the plane higher.
3. **Thrust** from the engine propels the plane forward.
4. **Drag**, wind resistance, holds the plane back.

When these four forces are balanced, the plane can cruise in a level direction.

Now, let's look at a model airplane and how it counteracts these forces. The illustration below shows the main parts of an airplane's structure.

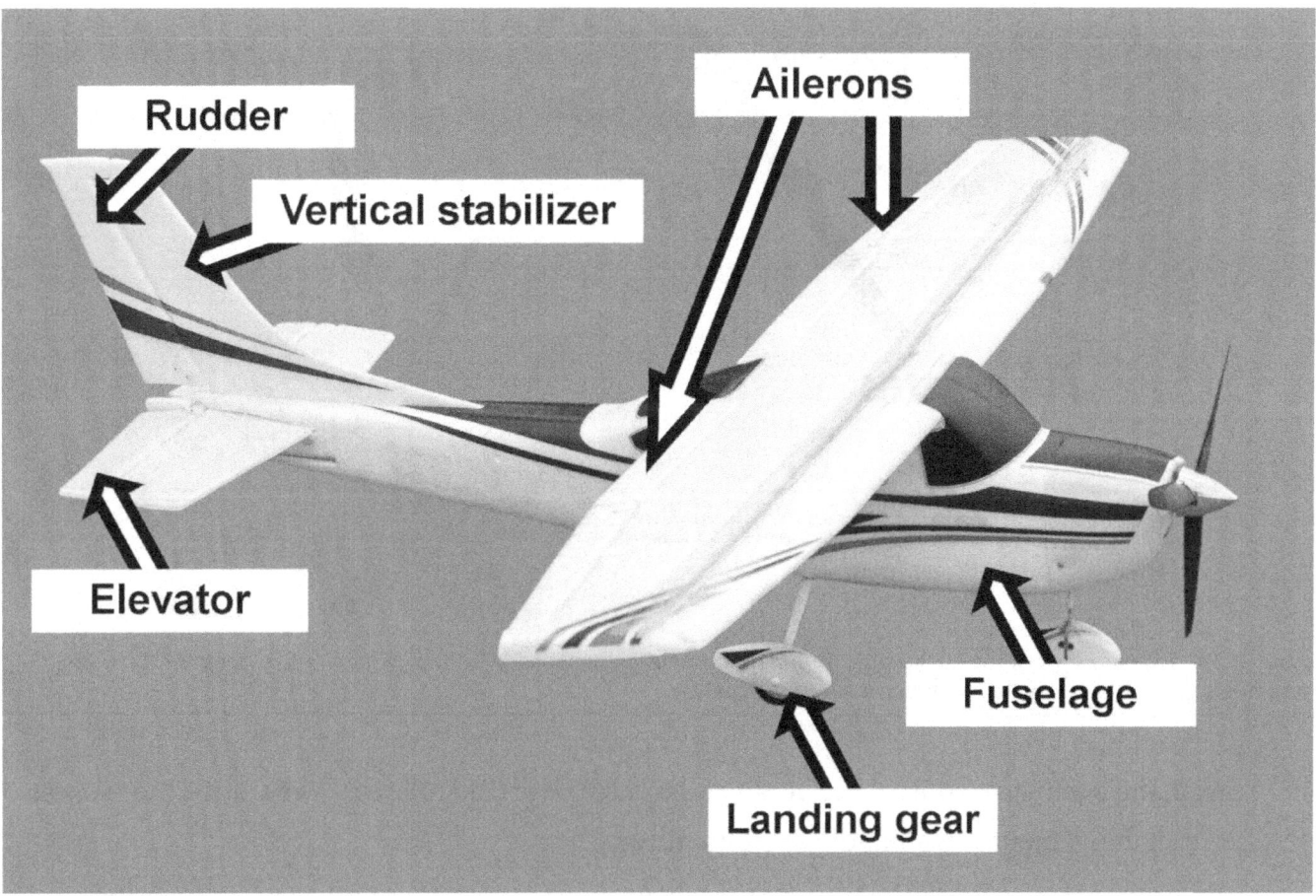

Above: The structure of a typical airplane.

Rudder: The trailing edge of the rudder moves left or right to control the lateral position of the nose of the aircraft.

Elevator: This surface moves up and down during flight to make the plane's nose point up or down. In conjunction with the ailerons, the elevator helps the plane turn.

Vertical stabilizer: A fixed surface to provide stability and keep the plane flying straight.

Ailerons: Hinged surfaces on the trailing edges of wings that make the aircraft bank. To roll left, the left aileron rises, and the right aileron lowers.

Fuselage: Main body.

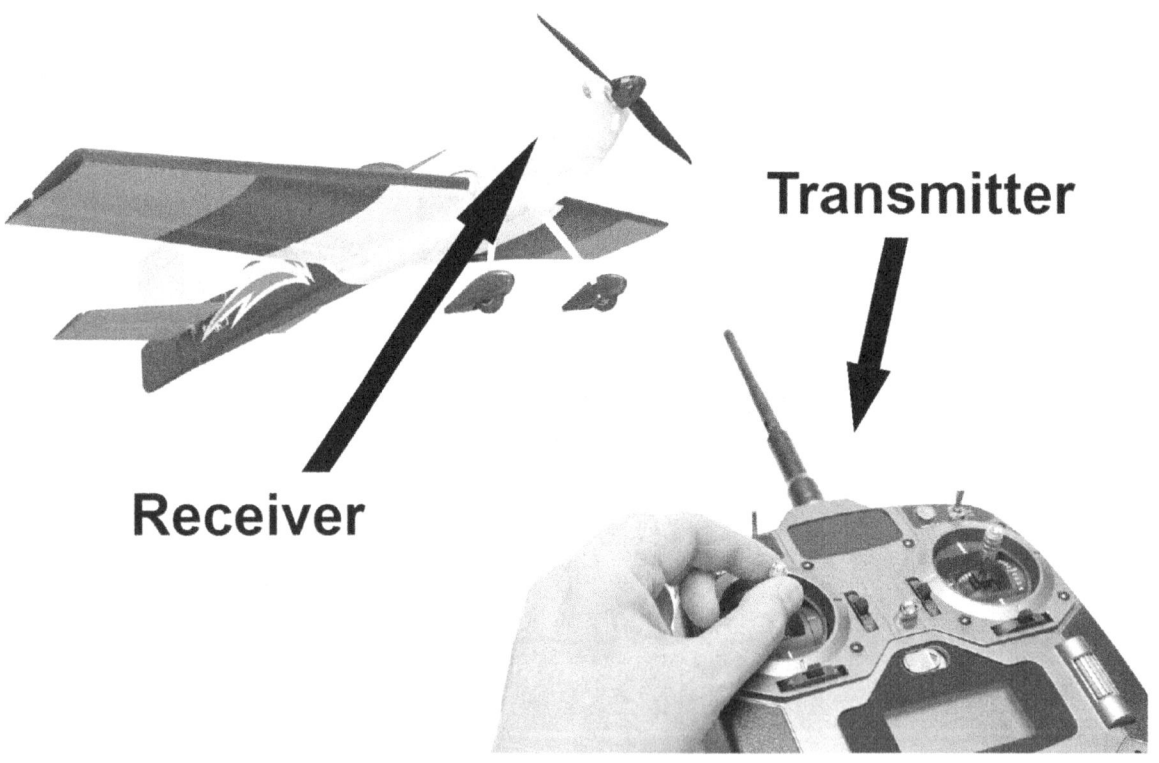

Above: The RC pilot moves the sticks on a transmitter, sometimes called a "radio," which relays commands to the airplane's control surface via an onboard wireless receiver.

Your plane's movable control surfaces—rudder, elevator and ailerons—are moved in response to your stick movements on a handheld transmitter.

Next, we'll look at a list of the best planes for RC beginners. Then we'll explore how a pilot actually flies the plane

One more thing before we get started: If you have any questions about getting started with RC flying, please send me an email at steve@weberbooks.com .

Okay, let's get started!

▶ THE FIVE BEST BEGINNER PLANES

Through trial and error, I've discovered which planes are the best for novice RC pilots. There are dozens of choices, but relatively few have earned a place in this book. I've purchased and flown all of the planes mentioned here (along with other planes that didn't make it into this book). My recommendations are based solely on how the planes perform, the quality of the materials, and the manufacturer's customer support. I received no compensation or samples from any of the companies mentioned.

You'll notice that most of the planes recommended in this section have a similar, classic design. They're inherently easy to fly because of these characteristics:

- A high wing, situated above a "cockpit" area, which makes the plane self-righting, meaning that it naturally settles into a stable cruise. (Harder-to-fly sport planes often have wings mounted on the bottom of the fuselage.)
- The angle of the wings forms a V shape—the wingtips are higher than the middle area. This wing design is called "dihedral," which further enhances stability.
- An airfoil, or the shape of the wing, provides lift. The top of the wing is curved, which makes the air rush over it faster. The bottom of the wing is flat, and the slower-moving air increases pressure, providing lift.

These planes fly relatively slow and are easy to control, so you'll have time to react and avoid trouble. They're also suitable for flying in a relatively small area—a backyard perhaps, or even indoors in a gymnasium. However, for your first flight, it's best to fly in a much larger area—a soccer field or larger area of at least 300 feet in diameter—to allow for mistakes.

Another advantage of starting with a small, slow plane is that, in the event of a crash, the risk of property damage or physical injury is very low. Because these planes are so small and weigh only an ounce or two, the force of an impact is slight. And since these planes are inexpensive to begin with, their loss or destruction isn't as painful as with a bigger, pricier airplane.

Another common denominator among my recommended planes: most have crash-avoidance technology, which helps prevent and correct some of the mistakes of inexperienced pilots. This technology costs extra, but it's well worth it, especially for new RC hobbyists. It can literally save your plane, more than once, every single time you go flying.

The SAFE system (Sensor-Assisted Flight Envelope) is the anti-crash technology included in several of my recommended planes. When it's needed, SAFE can rescue your plane from dangerous situations, such as a dive or spiral. You'll need to carefully read your plane's owner's manual to learn how to use SAFE with your particular plane and transmitter.

Consider this: would you buy a car that costs $50 less if it came without seatbelts or airbags? I doubt it.

The smaller "micro" planes usually don't have anti-crash technology; it's not practical for planes that small. Luckily, these lightweight planes will usually survive a crash unscathed because they don't build up enough inertia during flight to get damaged from a crash.

Ready-to-Fly vs. Bind-n-fly

Many of the planes designed for beginners are advertised as ready-to-fly, which means they come pre-assembled (or very nearly so) and everything you need is included—a battery, a battery charger, and a transmitter. All the components are factory-installed. Ready-to-fly outfits offer convenience and value. You don't have to worry about shopping for a motor, a battery, a receiver and transmitter—you just open the box, screw or tape a few parts together, and you can be in the air within an hour or so.

Some models are offered as "bind-n-fly," which means everything is included except a transmitter. So if you already have a transmitter, perhaps from another plane, you can bind the new plane to your existing receiver and avoid the expense of buying another transmitter.

Some beginner planes, advertised as "almost ready to fly," require an hour or more of assembly. Plane "kits" require more assembly, and might not include essential components like a motor or power system.

Yet another term you'll come across is "plug-n-play." This usually means that the airplane includes everything except a receiver and battery. In this case, you'll need to shop for the manufacturer's recommended receiver and install it yourself.

Most of the planes featured in this section are available at larger hobby shops. To find a nearby retailer, consult this page: http://www.modelaircraft.org/hobbyshopsearch.aspx .

With no further ado, here are your plane recommendations. Drum roll, please!

HobbyZone Champ

Retail price: $89.99 for ready-to-fly

Pluses: Low cost, slow flight, durable. High-wing "trainer" design aids stability

Minuses: Can't penetrate stiff winds

Wingspan: 22.4 inches

Length: 14.3 inches

Channels: Three (throttle, rudder, elevator)

Battery: 3.7V 1S 150mAh Li-Po (charger included)

Flying duration: 6 minutes

Flying weight: 1.3 ounces

Manufacturer: HobbyZone

Above: The Champ has the shape of a classic trainer aircraft. Copyright HobbyZone.

The Champ is the best-selling RC airplane for several years running. For less than $90, you get the complete beginner's package: a pre-assembled plane, battery, transmitter and charger. Within 15 minutes of opening the box, you could be teaching yourself how to fly in your back yard or local park.

Because of its tiny battery and motor, the Champ flies relatively slowly, and that's a good thing for new pilots. As the plane cruises around your flying area, you'll have plenty of time to figure out your next maneuver. If you make a mistake and point the plane in the wrong direction, you'll have plenty of time to adjust course.

If you have a large flying field, it's possible to teach yourself to fly with the Champ. But if your space is limited, practicing on a simulator is smart, so that you learn the basic flying maneuvers before risking a plane. The Champ was the first RC plane I flew, and I lost three of them during my first two weeks. Twice I got disoriented when the plane was high above my head. I panicked, pushed the transmitter sticks the wrong way, and lost my first two Champs in the woods near my house. My third Champ was blown away by a strong gust of wind, again stuck in a tree. After I lost that third Champ (and crashed a larger plane during its first flight), I finally buckled down, purchased a flight simulator, and learned to fly.

The story of my three lost Champs perfectly illustrates the strengths and weaknesses of the Champ (and similar small planes). First, the plane's light weight (just 1.3 ounces including flight battery) allows it to escape most crashes unscathed. You can ram a Champ full-speed into the ground or against a brick wall, and it will likely emerge with only superficial scuffs and scratches. Because of the plane's light weight, it has little inertia even at full speed, so a crash usually results in a harmless bounce. (If a curious child picks up and squeezes your Champ, however, the result can be catastrophic.)

The disadvantage of the Champ's low mass is that it can't penetrate even the lightest wind. If you try flying your Champ in breezy weather, you'll spend the entire time fighting against the wind rather than enjoying your flight.

Another knock against the Champ is that the included transmitter is a low-powered model that doesn't have much range. Although you can use it with other small planes, its short range limits you to backyards and small parks.

Even though the Champ is just a three-channel plane (throttle, rudder, and elevator), the rudder is controlled from the stick on the right-hand side of the transmitter, which simulates the control you'll have in the future from the ailerons on bigger, more full-featured planes.

HobbyZone Duet

Retail price: $59.99

Pluses: Very low cost and good value for the money; slow, predictable flight

Minuses: Transmitter can't be used with other planes; throttle lacks power

Wingspan: 20.6 inches

Length: 14.5 inches

Channels: Three—throttle, elevator, and yaw control from differential thrust from twin propellers

Battery: 150mAh 1S Li-Po (charger included)

Flying duration: 10 minutes

Flying weight: 1.34 ounces

Manufacturer: HobbyZone

Above: The Duet is a tiny aircraft with twin propellers. Copyright HobbyZone.

Some people consider the Duet more of a toy than a real RC plane. It costs just $60, and its transmitter is a cheapie that won't work with other planes (the Champ, which costs $30 more, has a transmitter you can bind and use with other small aircraft). Likewise, if you already have a favorite full-size transmitter you're using with other planes, you won't be able to bind it to the Duet because the receiver isn't compatible.

On the positive side, the Duet is an easy-to-fly trainer that lets the budding RC pilot enter the hobby for a rock-bottom price and get a taste of flying without the worry of crashing a more expensive plane. If you're susceptible to the RC flying bug, the Duet will confirm it for you.

The designers of the Duet kept its price low by keeping the plane's hardware simple—the Duet has no rudder or ailerons. Instead, the Duet uses differential thrust from its twin propellers to turn left or right. The simple design also provides an element of safety: since the propellers are mounted back on the Duet's wings, a nose-first crash will likely result in a harmless bounce and no damage to the propellers.

The Duet has small landing gear and rolls quite well on hard surfaces, but if you're flying on a grass field, the small wheels can get stuck. In that case, simply remove the wheels—you can hand-launch the plane and belly-land with ease.

The Duet can fly for a generous 10 minutes with its tiny one-cell battery. With its slow, easily controlled flight and whisper-quiet power system, the Duet is one plane that truly qualifies as a backyard flyer—just be sure to avoid the trees. During the winter months, you could fly your Duet indoors if you have access to a gymnasium or other large structure.

Although the Champ sells at a faster clip, many fans claim that the Duet is the perfect beginner plane.

My main gripe about the Duet is that it just doesn't have enough climbing power. With a freshly charged battery, this plane struggles to rise above 75 feet, so you can never quite get into a comfortable cruising mode. So this is a plane that the frequent flyer will likely grow out of within a week or two.

HobbyZone Sport Cub S with SAFE Technology

Retail price: $129.99 (Bind-n-fly version is $99.99)

Pluses: Easy-to-fly trainer; lowest-priced plane that includes SAFE technology

Minuses: Plane's light weight means it gets bounced around by stiff breezes

Wingspan: 24.3 inches

Length: 16.3 inches

Channels: Four – throttle, rudder, elevator and aileron

Battery: 3.7V 1S 150mAh Li-Po

Flying duration: 10 minutes

Flying weight: 2 ounces

Manufacturer: HobbyZone

Above: The Sport Cub is a great introduction to four-channel RC flying. Copyright HobbyZone.

The Sport Cub is an easy-to-fly trainer and the lowest-priced plane you'll find with SAFE technology, which can bail you out of dangerous situations. This plane is about 25 percent bigger and heavier than the Champ, and it has ailerons, so it's a nice step up. In my opinion, the Sport Cub, because of its several added features, is a more compelling choice as a first plane compared to the Champ, despite the $40 price difference.

Although it uses a small one-cell battery, the Sport Cub S has been designed to work with some accessories that smaller planes like the Champ can't handle. You can get a set of floats to make the plane capable of taking off and landing on water, and there's an optional onboard camera sold separately by HobbyZone. For more information, see the "Accessories" chapter in this book.

The Sport Cub S comes with a handy battery charger that plugs into a computer USB port.

This plane is capable of flying in relatively small spaces, such as a field 300 feet in diameter, and it has a steerable tail wheel for controlling taxi direction.

UMX Radian

Retail price: $89.99 (available as bind-n-fly only)

Pluses: Easy-to-fly, efficient airplane, provides lots of flying enjoyment out of a little battery; AS3X technology helps smooth flight during gusty conditions

Minuses: Can struggle in high winds, like other lightweight planes

Wingspan: 28.7 inches

Length: 16.5 inches

Channels: Three – throttle, rudder, and elevator

Battery: 1S 3.7V 150mAh 25C LiPo

Flying duration: 8 to 12 minutes in calm wind, at least 15 minutes when soaring with thermals

Flying weight: 1.5 ounces

Manufacturer: E-flite

Above: The UMX Radian is an inexpensive way to enter the entertaining world of sailplanes. Copyright E-flite.

The UMX Radian delivers more bang for your buck than any RC plane, in my opinion. It destroys the myth among some RC enthusiasts that you need a big, powerful plane to have fun. The little Radian uses the same type of one-cell battery as the Champ, for example, but the Radian can fly higher, farther and faster. Within a few minutes of launching this plane from your hand, the UMX Radian can be so high it's nearly out of sight. Once it's up there, the fun begins—

you can hunt for thermals like a hawk, cruise for a few minutes, dive back down, then climb back up to altitude, then do it all over again two or three times, for as long as 12 minutes. Whenever the battery runs short, you just glide to a belly landing.

For a tiny plane, the UMX Radian is surprisingly efficient. The flexible propeller folds up against the fuselage when the motor isn't running, keeping drag to a minimum. This plane also includes the AS3X stabilization technology, which smoothes out turbulence, giving the UMX Radian the feel of a much larger plane.

Another plus: this little guy can withstand some hard knocks. A full-speed crash into the ground or a brick wall is usually no big deal. You're more likely to damage this plane by accidentally sitting on it during your trip to the flying field.

Like other sailplanes, the little Radian is prone to "porpoising" (bobbing up and down between a near-stall and a short dive) if the center of gravity gets too far toward the tail. To remedy this, slide the battery toward the nose.

The manufacturer says this plane is intended for "intermediate" pilots, but I believe the UMX Radian can serve as a great first airplane. It's also fun enough to fly for experienced pilots to enjoy, too. The UMX Radian was one of the first planes I bought, but remains a favorite—it's usually with me on every trip to the flying field.

Once you're proficient at controlling the UMX Radian, you can have an hour's worth of fun with four little batteries in a relatively small flying area. It's simply amazing that a relatively new, amateur pilot can send the little 1.5-ounce UMX Radian to hundreds of feet in the air, then land it on a dime, even in breezy conditions.

Delta Ray with SAFE technology

Retail price: $179.99 (Available as Bind-n-fly, $149.99)

Pluses: Steady flight in low winds, capable of slow flight. SAFE technology can bail out new pilots.

Minuses: Uses older-technology brushed motors, subject to wear; can be hard to turn into the wind during breezy weather

Wingspan: 34 inches

Length: 31.8 inches

Channels: Four – throttle, ailerons/elevator on trailing edge of wings, and rudder control from differential thrust

Battery: 7.4V 2S 1300mAh 20C Li-Po (included) (charger included)

Flying duration: 8 minutes

Flying weight: 17.6 ounces

Manufacturer: HobbyZone

Above: The Delta Ray is a variation on the "flying wing" concept.

Although it's classified as an easy-to-learn trainer aircraft, the Delta Ray has a more exciting design than your typical trainer. No, this isn't your grandpa's airplane—the Delta Ray looks like something out of *Star Wars*. There's no fuselage, just a nose cone and one giant wing and tail fin.

The Delta Ray is right in the middle between a recommended first plane and recommended second plane. Pilots who buy this plane tend to love it and keep flying it for a long time without growing bored with it.

The SAFE technology provides a progressive learning experience, allowing beginning pilots to "grow into" the plane. As with other planes equipped with SAFE, the "panic button" quickly rights the plane if the pilot becomes disoriented. In all flight modes, the AS3X technology helps smooth handling in turbulent weather.

The ready-to-fly Delta Ray requires some minor assembly that will consume about 30 minutes—attaching the wingtips and landing gear. No tools are required except for a small Phillips screwdriver and the included pre-cut tape.

Unlike most RC planes, the Delta Ray has no rudder. Yaw is controlled by differential thrust between the twin propellers (when the rudder control is activated, the propellers move at differing speeds, pulling the model to one side or the other).

Despite its aggressive-looking profile, the Delta Ray can cruise at nice, slow speeds (pull the throttle stick back to about 35% and provide a little up-elevator), which is a tremendous help to new pilots.

In breezy conditions it can be difficult to turn the Delta Ray into the wind. So I prefer flying this plane on "high rates." This is a setting on the transmitter, usually a switch on the top-right corner that increases the "throw" distance on the plane's control surfaces.

The ready-to-fly Delta Ray comes with a DX4e four-channel DSMX transmitter.

The Delta Ray is easy to transport. It's not a small plane, yet you can stow the Delta Ray in the trunk of your car, drive to the flying field, and get airborne without having to attach a wing. It's easy to pop in a fresh battery under the hatch on the bottom of the aircraft.

Overall it's a nice plane, but the Delta Ray is a little underpowered for my taste. For another $100 or so, you can step up to the E-Flite Apprentice (reviewed in the next section), which offers more speed and power, a more efficient brushless motor, and the ability to fly in windier conditions. If you're considering the Delta Ray as a second plane, I would suspect you'd be happier with the Apprentice.

Recommended Second Planes

The planes I recommend in this section are quite easy to fly, and technically could serve as a first plane for a pilot with extensive experience on a simulator. But they do represent a step up in expense, power, and speed, so I hesitate to recommend them to new pilots. These planes fly much faster than ultra-micros like the HobbyZone Champ.

Apprentice 15e with SAFE technology

Retail price: $299.99 as Ready-to-Fly; $269.99 as Bind-n-fly

Pluses: Rock solid, stable airplane; SAFE system can bail you out of trouble if you become disoriented

Minuses: It's hard to find any faults with this plane. To nitpick, it's difficult to install the front landing gear because it requires removing the cowl and propeller – which calls for a socket wrench and a very strong wrist.

Wingspan: 59 inches

Length: 42.5 inches

Channels: Four – throttle, rudder, elevator and ailerons

Battery: 11.1V 3S 3200mAh LiPo

Flying duration: 14 minutes

Flying weight: 49 ounces

Manufacturer: E-flite

Above: The Apprentice is a trainer, but it remains a favorite plane of many intermediate and advanced fliers.

The Apprentice is a well-designed trainer plane. Its high-wing, dihedral design makes it awfully easy to fly. Yet this is an athletic plane with plenty of power, so you won't grow bored with it in a matter of weeks, as you might with a micro plane. You can fly this plane hard, diving, looping and rolling, and its beefy battery will keep you in the air for 13 to 15 minutes.

This plane's SAFE system makes taking off and landing easy if you're using the "beginner" flight mode. This plane is relatively heavy, so landing hard on the nose wheel can damage it.

Until you're already proficient at soft landings, use the "beginner" mode during landings, which helps keep the plane level.

The manufacturer classifies the Apprentice as a "beginner" plane, but a pilot shouldn't try flying this one without experience with smaller planes and, if possible, a simulator. The Apprentice can be intimidating because it flies so much faster than the micro planes. For example, I bought an Apprentice as my second plane after cutting my teeth on multiple HobbyZone Champs. Technically, I had the skill to fly the Apprentice but I didn't have the confidence to immediately take it up to a safe altitude (100 or 150 feet) during my first flight. During my first flight, I was timid with the sticks, nervous of crashing my brand-new $300 airplane. As a result, within 30 seconds I rammed my pristine Apprentice into the metal edge of a soccer goal, cracking the wing, fuselage, and cowl. Luckily, I was able to repair the damage with glue and tape, but it could have been much worse—the heavier the plane, the more severe crash damage tends to be.

Several flights with the Apprentice will give you confidence to try some aerobatic maneuvers. Whenever I take my Apprentice to the flying field, I bring along three batteries, which ensures a solid 45 minutes of fun.

Parkzone Radian

Retail price: $249.99 ready-to-fly ($159.99 for plug-n-play version (requires receiver and transmitter)

Pluses: Easy to fly, one battery can provide an hour or more of flying time

Minuses: Nose-first landings can cause major damage to the fuselage and wings

Wingspan: 78 inches

Length: 44.7 inches

Channels: Three – throttle, rudder, and elevator

Battery: 11.1V 1300mAh Li-Po

Flying duration: 15 minutes to an hour or more

Flying weight: 30 ounces

Manufacturer: Parkzone

The Radian is truly a majestic sight—the way it soars through the sky with its 78-inch wingspan is simply breathtaking.

This plane is the larger version of the UMX Radian small-powered sailplane mentioned in the previous section. And this one is easy to fly, just like its little brother. But unlike the small Radian, hard landings can result in grave damage to the Parkzone Radian. Two vulnerable areas are the thin areas of the fuselage—the rear part near the tail, and the middle part where the wings attach. Land this plane hard on its nose—or clip a wing at moderate speed—and you'll likely break the fuselage in one or more places. So although many folks consider this a "beginner" plane, it's too easy to suffer a demoralizing crash on your first or second flight. And in any case, I don't recommend putting a $250 plane at risk until you've got some flying time under your belt.

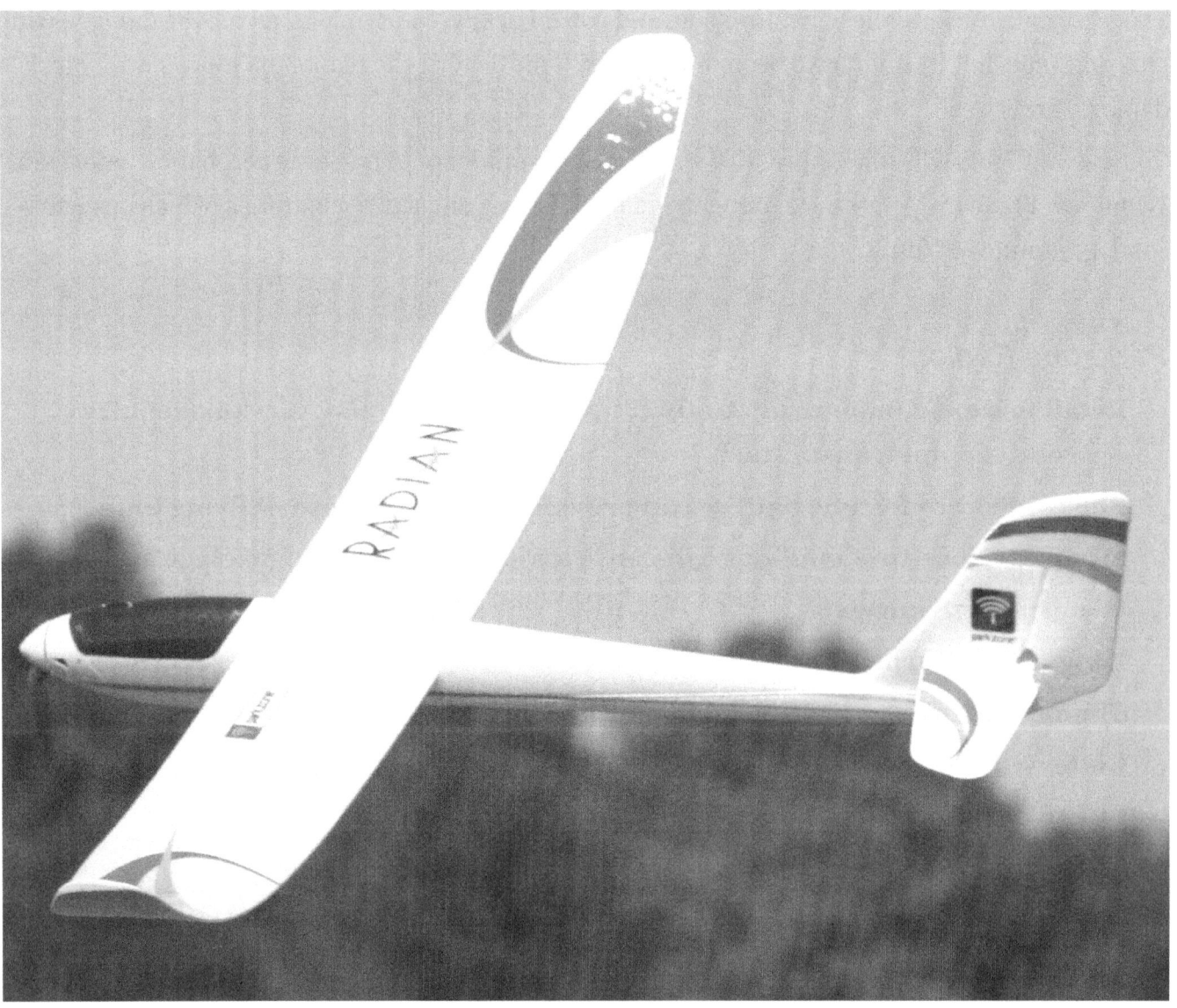

Above: The Radian powered glider has an awesome 78-inch wingspan. Copyright Parkzone.

The Radian has fantastic glide performance—the plane keeps going and going—but that makes it a challenge to land. So, for the first several times you fly it, I suggest you restrict yourself to a field where you'll have at least 100 yards to land.

Unlike most large planes, the Radian can fly quite slowly, and its wing design (polyhedral) tends to make it self-righting—bank the plane left or right, let go of the sticks, and it will straighten back out all by itself. This plane's huge wingspan and smart design makes it ultra-efficient. Under favorable wind conditions, you can enjoy flights of an hour or more despite this plane's relatively small battery.

Parkzone Sport Cub

Retail price: $219.99 for bind-n-fly ($179.99 for plug-n-play)

Pluses: Easy-to-fly trainer; includes AS3X stabilization technology

Minuses: The wing struts give the plane a scale look but are cumbersome if you need to remove the wing for transport

Wingspan: 51 inches

Length: 34 inches

Channels: Four—throttle, aileron, elevator, rudder, telemetry; requires an optional servo for flaps

Battery: 11.1V 3S 1300mAH LiPo

Flying duration: About 6 minutes

Flying weight: 33.3 ounces

Manufacturer: Parkzone

The Parkzone Sport Cub is a big plane, and it looks very realistic in flight. Unfortunately, the downside of all that heft is short flight durations—just four to seven minutes, depending on how liberal you are with the throttle. To me, that's a big disappointment; it's not nearly enough time for a fun flight. So my suggestion is to upgrade to a 2,200 mAh battery. You'll get flight times of 10 minutes, and the battery's extra weight is no problem.

The Sport Cub comes with an installed six-channel receiver with built-in AS3X stabilization technology.

The Cub has oversized, fat tires to make grass landings easier, and there's a steerable tail wheel for controlling taxi direction.

Above: The Sport Cub hits the sweet spot in terms of scale appearance, size, and price. Copyright Parkzone.

One thing that annoys me about this Cub—and similar planes—is the wing struts, which connect the wing to the bottom of the fuselage. Yes, they help make this scale-looking plane more realistic, but in practical terms they get in the way. For transportation and storage, it's not as easy to pop wings on and off when struts are involved.

This Cub is a big improvement over a previous model called the Super Cub S, which had some design flaws and tended to get knocked around by moderate winds.

ParkZone T-28 Trojan

Retail price: $249.99 for Ready-to-Fly; $239.99 for Bind-n-fly; $179.99 for Plug-n-Play

Pluses: Stable, easy-to-fly plane with aerobatic capability

Minuses: Although this is a well-mannered airplane, it debuted several years ago and does not feature the newer stabilization or SAFE technologies.

Wingspan: 44 inches

Length: 36 inches

Channels: Four – throttle, ailerons, rudder, elevator

Battery: 11.1V 3S 1800mAh Li-Po

Flying duration: 12 minutes

Flying weight: 30 ounces

Manufacturer: Parkzone

Above: The T-28 is available in two paint schemes—the red and white Navy style, shown here, and a silver and blue Air Force style.

This is a scale reproduction of the military trainer used during the 1950s through the early 1970s. It has a peppy motor that can make this plane climb impressively. A lot of people who buy this plane marvel at its good combination of flying characteristics—stable and easy-to-fly, yet powerfully aerobatic. The adage "it flies like it's on rails" applies. This has been a very popular plane for several years; there's almost always at least one T-28 at a club field. One downside is this model hasn't been updated with the newest stabilization and anti-crash technologies, ASX3 and SAFE. However, there is a relatively simple way to update the T-28 electronics: You can buy the plug-n-play version of the T-28 and install a SAFE receiver, which costs about $110. (For more information on installing a SAFE receiver on this or other planes, see this page: http://bit.ly/1so4C4F .)

This plane is very maneuverable—too maneuverable for inexperienced pilots. This is a low-wing plane with the potential to get you in trouble in a hurry.

Great Planes ElectriFly EP Super Sportster

Retail price: $129.99 for plug-n-play

Pluses: Sporty performance from low-wing design; great value

Minuses: Firewall and landing gear tend to come loose after hard landings, but some glue takes care of the issue

Wingspan: 40 inches

Length: 32.5 inches

Channels: Four – throttle, ailerons, rudder, elevator

Battery: 3S 11.1V 1300mAh 25C LiPo

Flying duration: 12 minutes

Flying weight: 22 ounces

Manufacturer: Great Planes Model Manufacturing

Above: The Super Sportster is a good introduction to four-channel flying. Copyright Great Planes Model Manufacturing.

This is an attractive, low wing sport plane that provides a good introduction to sport flying and aerobatics. It's made for maneuvers like loops, rolls, snap rolls and spins, but it's almost easy enough to fly to qualify as a solid choice for a first plane. This plane has no bad tendencies—it flies rather like a Parkzone T-28 but a little faster and more aerobatic. It's a solid choice for new intermediate pilots.

DHC-2 Beaver

Retail price: $299.97 for ready-to-fly ($209.97 without transmitter)

Pluses: Outstanding construction and attention to detail; plane has plenty of power and is fun to fly.

Minuses: Hard to transport because wings are cumbersome to remove

Wingspan: 59 inches

Length: 38.5 inches

Channels: Five – throttle, rudder, ailerons, elevator, flaps

Battery: 11.1V 1800mAh LiPo

Flying duration: 12 minutes

Flying weight: 48 ounces

Manufacturer: Flyzone

This scale model has been a popular one for many years, and the new edition has been updated with a new trim scheme, larger bush tires on the conventional landing gear, floats with water rudders, and working navigation and landing lights, which look impressive during late afternoon and dusk flights. This is a gorgeous plane, and during flight it closely resembles the real McCoy, which was produced until 1967. It was known primarily as a bush plane used for cargo and passenger hauling, crop dusting and aerial topdressing, and as a military utility aircraft. This is an elaborate, relatively complicated airplane, so it is extremely difficult to repair it in the event of a crash.

▶ TEACH YOURSELF TO FLY

The first part of flying is checking to be sure that your transmitter and airplane are responding as expected. Use the illustration below as a guide.

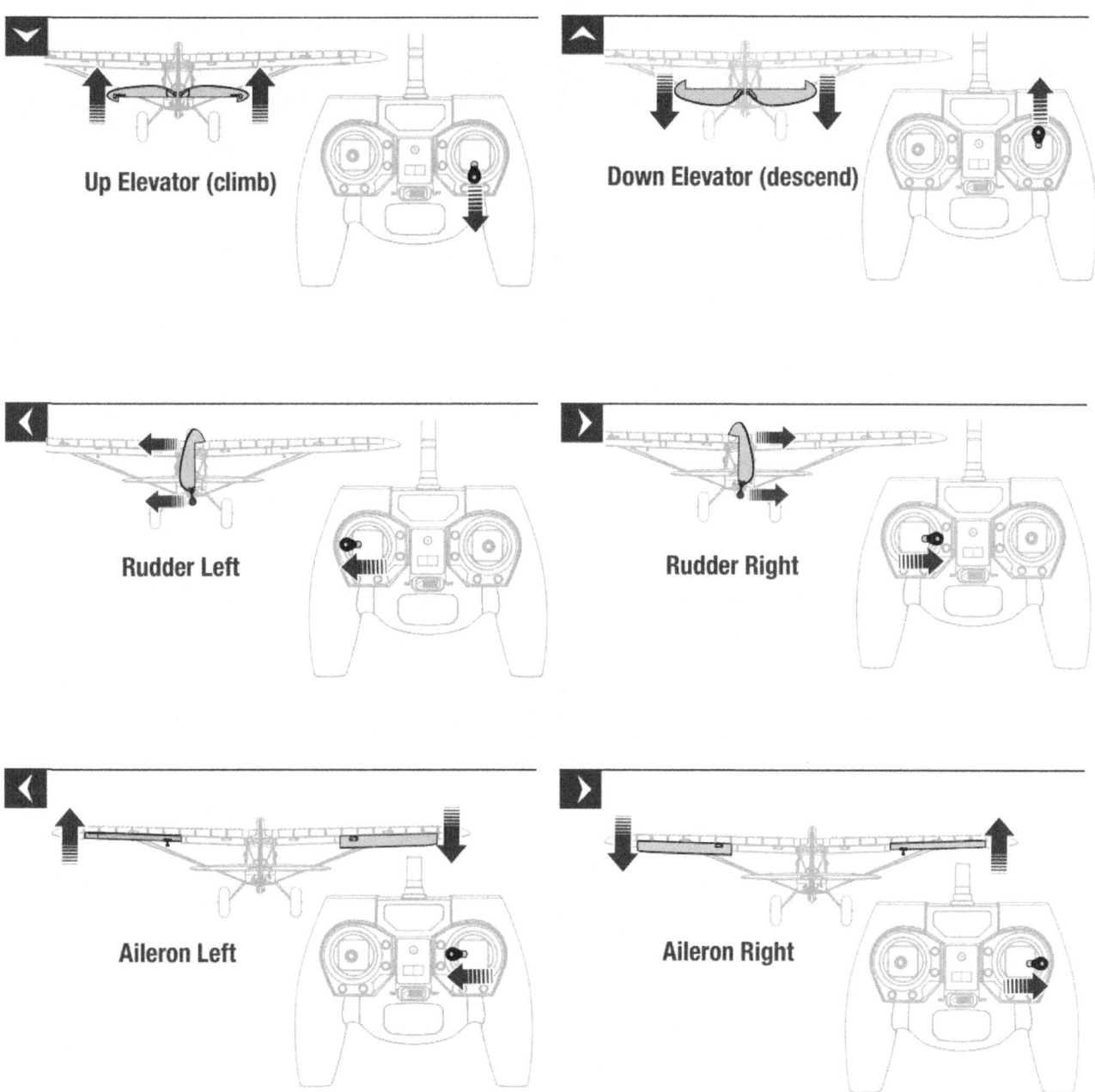

Above: A plane's control surfaces react to these commands from the pilot's transmitter. Copyright Horizon Hobby, Inc.

Range check: Before a model's first flight of the day, perform a range check. This is especially critical when flying a new model. To perform the check, walk about 100 feet away from your model, then verify that the plane's control surfaces respond appropriately to inputs from the transmitter.

Depending on the size of your plane, you may need an assistant to help you conduct a range check. If the plane doesn't respond as expected, do not fly it.

Control direction test: Move the sticks on your transmitter and ensure the aircraft responds appropriately as shown in the previous illustration. Restrain your model (by holding the back of the fuselage or placing your feet in front of both sides of the horizontal stabilizer) and check the throttle response. If your model doesn't respond as expected, do not fly it.

Taking Off

The first part of flying is fairly intuitive. Visualize yourself in the "cockpit" of your plane, looking forward.

Push the left stick forward to generate thrust from the propeller. With enough throttle, your aircraft will taxi forward (or, if already in flight, your aircraft with climb and add speed).

One cardinal rule of flying is that your plane should travel **into the wind** during takeoffs and landings. The reason: during takeoff, moving into the wind generates more lift, allowing your plane to climb faster and steadier. During landing, moving into the wind slows your plane's groundspeed, and makes it easier to land on the intended spot on the runway.

Most planes will take off from the runway at about 75 percent of full throttle. Pulling back gently on the right stick provides **up elevator** (which raises the trailing edge of the elevator and helps nudge the nose of your plane skyward.) But don't pull the stick back too far or your plane might stall. A stall is more likely at slow speeds while your nose is pointed too high, causing your plane to stop, then fall.

Flying Your Plane

After takeoff, climb about 100 to 150 feet in altitude, which is sometimes called "two or three mistakes high." If you make some errors in flight, you'll have time to recover before crashing into the ground.

Let's imagine we've just taken off and climbed above the runway. As the plane travels away from you, imagine you're in the cockpit. You're going to control the direction of the plane by pointing the nose of your aircraft in the direction you want to fly. You can make the following inputs. (The previous illustration helps illustrate these movements):

1. **Pull the right stick toward you to climb**: the nose will rise as the tail goes down. This is a result of the elevator's trailing edge moving up, also known as **up elevator**.
2. **Push the right stick away from you to descend**: the nose will drop as the tail moves up, resulting from the elevator's trailing edge moving down. Also known as **down elevator**.
3. **Push the right stick leftward to bank left**: The nose moves to the left, the aircraft banks left, resulting from the left aileron moving up, and the right aileron moving down. (On a plane with no ailerons, the turn is initiated by the rudder.)
4. **Push the right stick rightward to bank right**: The nose moves to the right and the aircraft banks right, resulting from the left aileron moving down, and the right aileron moving up.

Two movements of the left stick move the rudder:

5. **Push the left stick to the left**: The nose moves left, resulting from the trailing edge of the rudder moving left.
6. **Push the left stick right**: The nose moves right, resulting from the trailing edge of the rudder moving right.

Flying in an Oval Pattern

Start out simple. Begin flying in an oval pattern. After takeoff, fly in a straight line upwind, then turn 90 degrees counter-clockwise and proceed for the second leg of your pattern. Again, turn 90 degrees counterclockwise and proceed downwind. Line up with your initial leg and turn 90 degrees again.

Try to maintain a constant speed and altitude throughout your oval pattern. This means you'll have to pull back on the elevator as you're turning. To maintain a constant speed, you'll need to lower the throttle as you're flying with the wind, and raise the throttle when you're flying into the wind. Once you're mastered flying in a counter-clockwise oval pattern, try flying in the opposite direction—turning clockwise each turn.

With practice, you'll learn how to complete your turns gently without losing speed or altitude. The key is learning to apply the correct amount of up-elevator during your turn, in addition to ailerons or rudder.

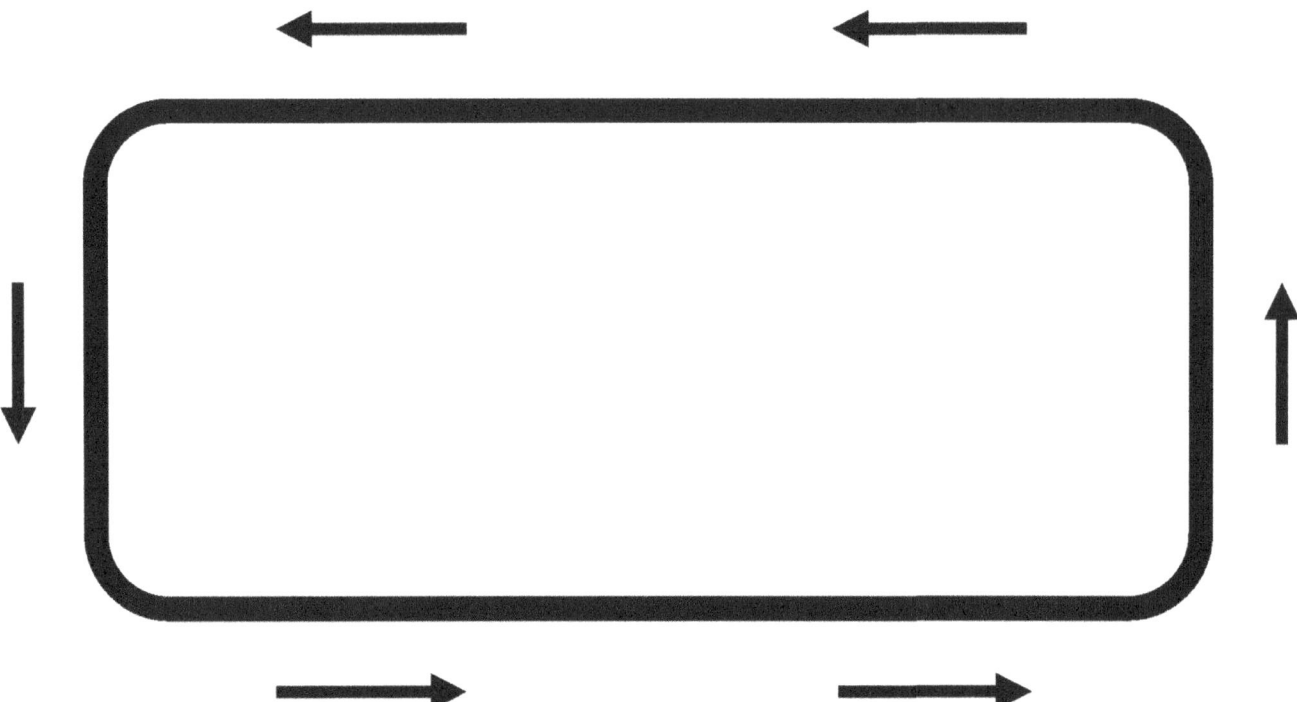

Above: A counter-clockwise oval flight pattern.

Once you're proficient at flying oval patterns, try flying figure eights. Again, try to maintain the same speed and altitude throughout the pattern. Figure eights are much harder than a simple oval. Don't worry if this takes several trips to the flying field—learning to fly properly takes lots of practice.

Resisting the Tendency to Overcorrect

One habit that afflicts most new pilots is their tendency to **overcorrect**. For example, when the new pilot sees his plane drifting to the right, his inclination is to push the right stick leftward, as far as it will go. His intention is to get the plane back on course as quickly as possible. Resist the urge to bang the stick all the way. Instead, use gentle, small stick movements—then your plane will be much easier to fly.

Banging the sticks all the way to one side is too drastic a movement—because the result is that the plane jerks too far in the intended direction. The next thing you know, you'll have to move the stick toward the right again—because you overcorrected to the left.

How can you learn to be gentle with the sticks? Here's a good mental exercise, based on a task you're probably familiar with—driving a car. Let's imagine you're behind the wheel, cruising down a straight highway. To stay in your lane, you periodically nudge the steering wheel left or right. If you're an experienced driver, it's second-nature—if the car drifts left, you nudge the wheel to the right a bit. It's a gentle, slight movement you perform without really thinking about it. Moving the steering wheel just a fraction of an inch every so often keeps your car on course. Try to control your plane in a similar fashion. Small inputs are usually all that's required. Most of your inputs on the sticks should be small—no more than the width of your thumb.

Controlling the Plane as It's Flying Toward You

We've just seen that flying while you're "behind" the plane is fairly intuitive—you simply point the nose of the plane in the direction you want it to go. Sooner or later, though, you've got to turn the plane around, and that's when things get confusing. While the plane's flying toward you, you've got to reverse your movement of the right stick. For example, instead of pointing the stick right to turn right, you point the stick left to make the plane turn right.

Here's a simple technique for learning to fly while the plane is coming toward you. Viewing the illustration below, imagine that the wing is a tabletop. Your task is to keep the "table" level. As you can see, the left side of the table is sloping downward. With your right stick, "prop up" the low part of the table—nudge your right stick leftward, toward the low point of the wing, and the plane will level.

Above: To level a plane that is banking while it's flying toward you, point your right stick toward the low part of the wing.

Landing the Airplane

Nothing makes a new pilot more nervous than landing. Remember, you'll land into the wind whenever possible, which will help provide more lift, keeping your aircraft steady. Also, the headwind makes the plane fly "slower" relative to the ground, giving you some margin for error.

On your last oval or two before landing, reduce the throttle to cut speed and altitude.

Line up with the runway on your final approach. Reduce the throttle further to bleed off speed and altitude. You'll want to fly as slowly as possible without putting yourself in danger of a stall. If your plane is equipped with SAFE technology, the "beginner" mode will help create ideal conditions for landing—keeping the plane's nose up and the wings level, with just enough throttle to keep the plane steady.

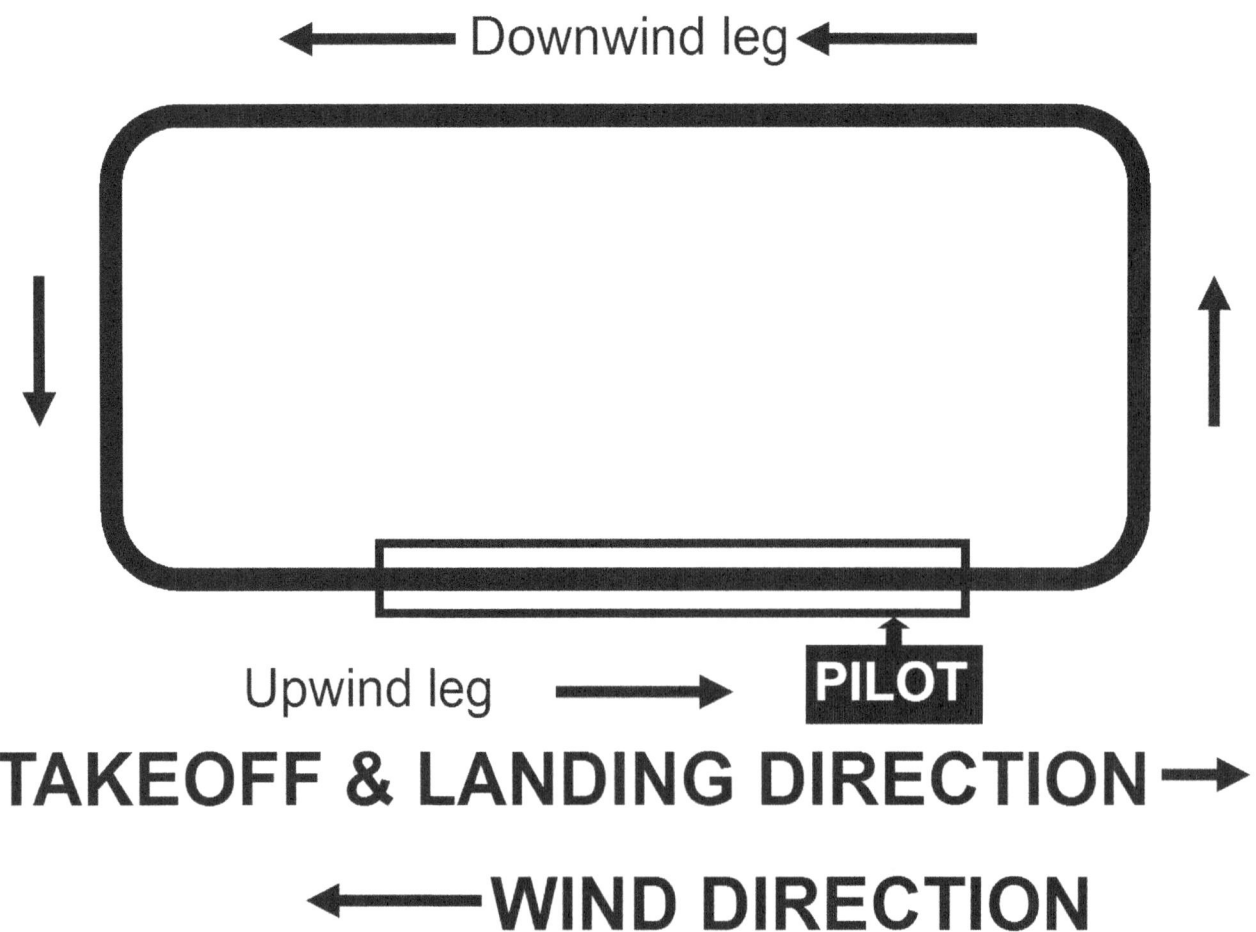

Again, here's our illustration of how stick movements affect our flight:

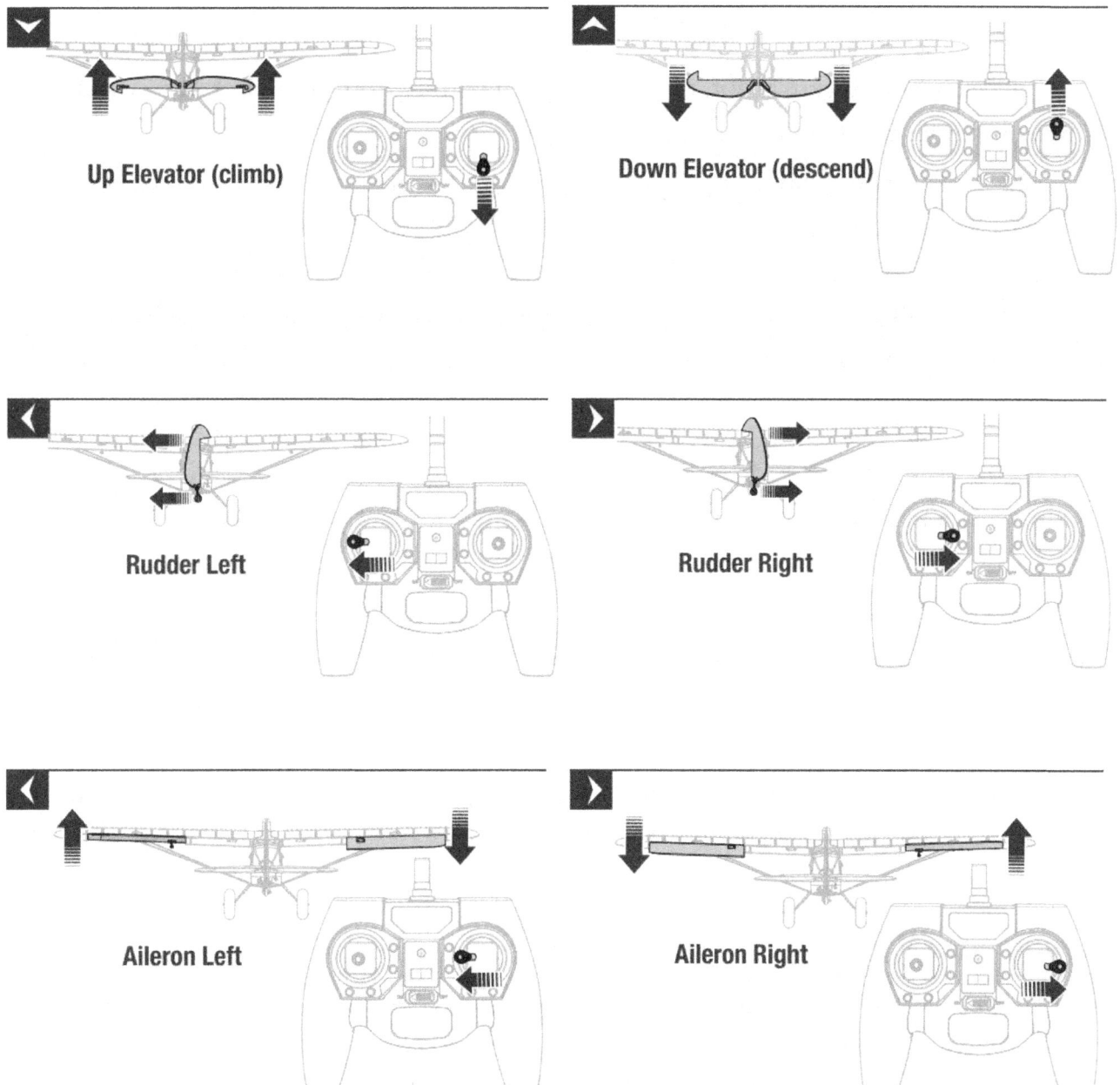

Flaring Your Plane for Touchdown

Just as your landing gear approaches the runway, give some **up elevator** by pulling back on the right stick. This will pitch your nose up, bleed off some more speed, and help ensure that your landing gear contacts the ground gently, simultaneously.

Always keep the plane in sight and upwind when possible. When the plane is upwind, you have more time to react to unexpected events.

It's easy to lose your plane if you take your eyes off it, even for an instant. Resist the urge to look down at your control sticks or to engage in conversation that includes eye contact.

After you've concluded your flight, remove the flight battery from your aircraft to avoid over-discharging batteries and risking permanent damage.

If your Li-Po battery discharges below a certain point, the receiver usually reduces power to the motor, known as a low-voltage cutoff (LVC). If you notice reduced motor power, or a pulsing of the motor, land as soon as possible. Although it might be possible to take off again with a battery drained to this point, don't be tempted—at the least, you might damage the battery, and at the worst, you could lose control of the plane and cause damage or injury.

Don't Fight the Weather

Windy conditions contribute to crashes and lost planes. Resist the urge to fly in breezy weather, particularly when you're first learning to fly. Winds of 15 miles per hour or more means it's not a good day for flying.

Most RC planes aren't waterproof, so don't fly in inclement weather, not even a light drizzle. If moisture from the ground adheres to your plane, wipe it dry as soon as possible.

It's best to store your plane and batteries at room temperature to ensure reliable operation. Always fly with fully charged batteries. Battery performance can deteriorate significantly during cold weather, so plan on reduced flight times when it's cold.

Trimming your Plane

Does your airplane tend to drift in a certain direction, even when the sticks are in neutral positions? If so, you may need to "trim" your plane. Modern transmitters have trim buttons, as illustrated in the drawing below. For example, let's imagine that your plane, while flying at a cruising speed, tends to sink toward the ground. You can adjust the rudder's default position by pressing the **elevator trim up button**. Your transmitter will emit a beeping sound each time you press the button, and the elevator will be adjusted accordingly, one small movement for each beep.

If necessary, adjust the trim for each control surface—elevator, rudder, and ailerons, until your plane flies true.

Sometimes your control surfaces will be so far out of alignment that you aren't able to correct the surface far enough with your transmitter's trim buttons. In that case you'll need to manually adjust the surfaces by disconnecting your surface's control-rod clevis and turning it clockwise or counter-clockwise, then reconnecting the linkage.

If you're having a hard time visualizing the trimming process, watch this video demonstration at Flitetest.com: http://youtu.be/gzCKEVP7VJQ .

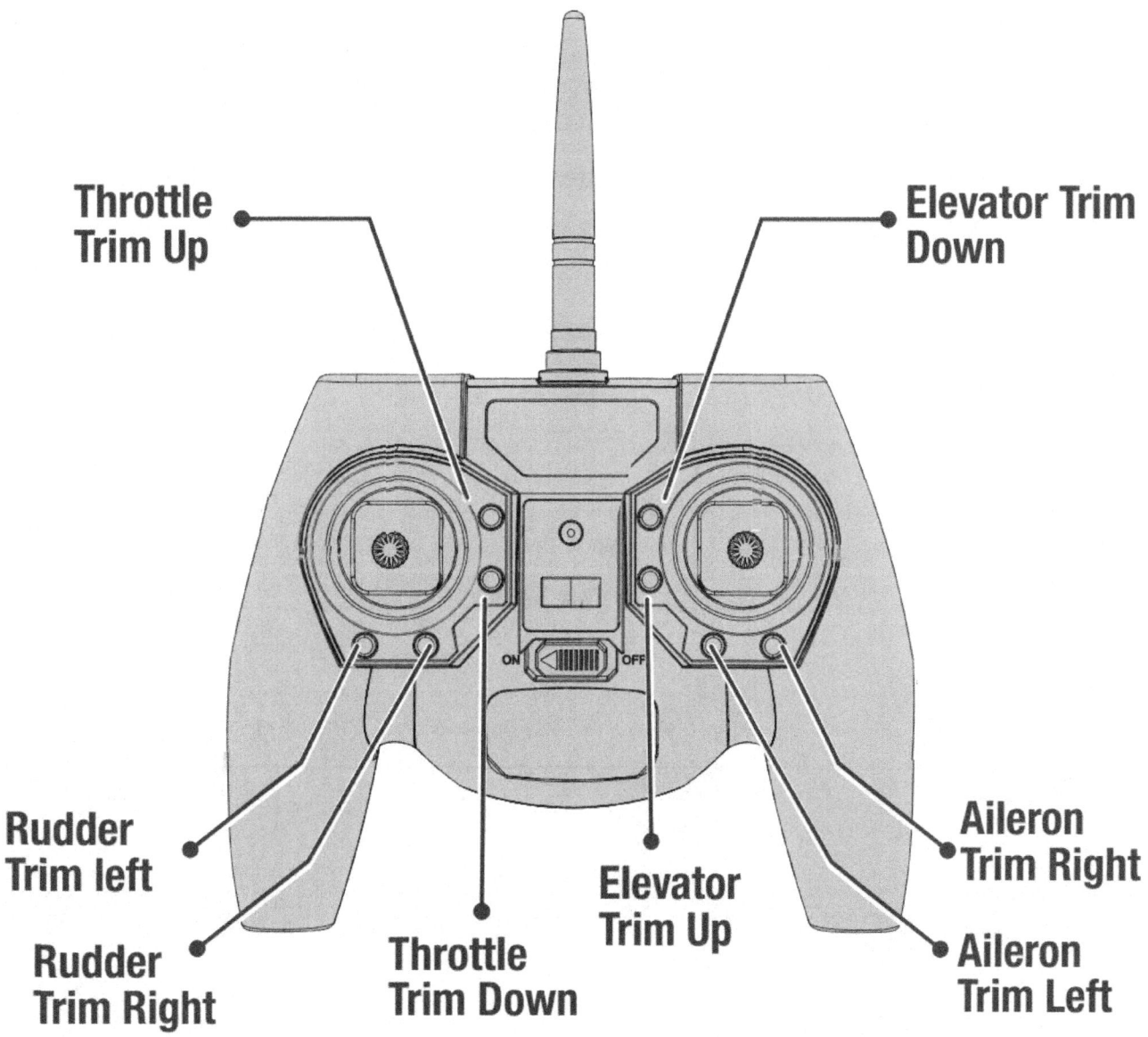

Above: Fine-tune the position of your plane's control surfaces by clicking on the transmitter's trim buttons.

Hand-launching Your Plane

Some planes don't have landing gear and are designed for hand launching. Sometimes the weather or field surface dictates a hand launch, even with a plane with landing gear. Here's how:

1. Grasp your plane under the fuselage with your dominant hand—with the arm you throw with. With your other hand, hold your transmitter.

2. With one of your fingers, move the left stick on the transmitter to 50 percent to 75 percent of throttle. (Some pilots use their teeth to move the stick.)

3. Toss your plane forward, into the wind, on an angle just slightly inclined from the ground.

With big, heavy planes, it helps to build momentum by striding forward with one of your feet.

Using a neck strap attached to your transmitter makes flying easier, especially during hand launches.

Above: Hand-launch your plane with a gentle toss and a bit of up-elevator.

Depending on the style of the model you're launching, you might need to modify your technique. To learn a variety of hand-launching techniques, view this video: http://youtu.be/S3H03qE9Tys .

Troubleshooting

With every plane you fly, you'll run into unforeseen problems. Oftentimes, the fix for a particular issue is amazingly simple. It just takes a little research and a process of elimination. Consider the possibilities below, and re-read your plane's owner's manual.

Aircraft propeller pulses

Receiver is loose. Tighten it.

Battery is discharged. Land immediately and completely charge battery.

Aircraft control surfaces are out of alignment

Use trim controls on transmitter. For further adjustments, manually adjust the clevis to adjust trim. (Turn clevis clockwise or counter-clockwise to adjust alignment.)

Aircraft doesn't respond to transmitter inputs

Double-check power on/off switches.

Check the connections in the aircraft's receiver.

Transmitter may be too close to aircraft, metal objects or wireless devices and cause interference. Aircraft may have to be re-bound to transmitter.

Ensure battery is fully charged.

Check for corrosion in battery compartment.

Aircraft climbs too steeply or stalls

Center of gravity is out of adjustment. Try moving battery toward the nose.

Throttle does not respond, but other controls work as expected.

Throttle trim may be too high. Adjust downward.

Motor may be disconnected.

Elevator or other surface oscillates or flutters during flight

You might be flying too fast. Slow down.

Ensure the surface's control arm is moving freely and is connected as indicated in the plane's manual.

Repairing Your Aircraft

Crashes are inevitable, but often you can repair a plane's molded Styrofoam parts with glue and tape. Be sure to use a foam-safe glue, as some formulations will melt Styrofoam. My favorite is Gorilla Glue, which dries fast and is amazingly strong. Be sure to get "White" Gorilla Glue, which dries white, instead of the standard formulation, which dries an ugly dark yellow. Also, be careful to apply Gorilla Glue sparingly—it foams and expands while drying, so if you apply too much, it can move the parts out of alignment. Another brand of glue that works well with foam RC models is "Foam Tac" by Beacon Adhesives. It works with Styrofoam, balsa wood, and carbon fiber. Unlike Gorilla Glue, Foam Tac doesn't foam and expand when it dries, and it stays flexible instead of becoming brittle.

Tape is the other major tool for crash repair. Clear packing tape, available at any office supply store, works for patching planes. Some proactive hobbyists apply a strip of tape to the leading edges of wings, which can reduce the damage in case the wing hits the ground or other obstacle.

Many foam planes have hinges made from a thin layer of foam—these are commonly used at the joint between an aileron and wing, or between the rudder or elevator and the stabilizer. Because the foam is very thin at the hinge, it's vulnerable to damage. Sometimes the hinge will rip apart during a hard landing; sometimes it simply comes apart after repeated use.

Fortunately, you can repair these hinges with two different materials: First, for a minor tear, you can use hinge tape—the leading brand is Du-Bro Electric Flyer Hinge Tape, which looks like regular Scotch tape but is more flexible. For bigger jobs—such as a completely detached rudder—try "Professional Welder Adhesive" by Homax. A thin layer of the stuff will provide a strong, yet flexible, bond. While the hinge dries, it helps to provide a brace to keep the joint aligned. Low-adhesion painter's masking tape will do the trick, keeping the joint aligned but not damaging the foam when it's removed. Here's a video demonstration of this hinge-repair technique: http://youtu.be/UmyqdMbVfok .

▶ ACCESSORIES BUYING GUIDE

You can greatly enhance your enjoyment of RC flying if you buy the right accessories. The problem is that beginners are faced with a bewildering array of choices. This section is devoted to helping you determine exactly which accessories are worth your money.

Computer Flight Simulator

A good flight simulator is worth its weight in gold. Learning the basic flying maneuvers on a simulator enables you to go to the flying field and proceed with confidence. The $100 or $200 you spend on a good simulator can pay for itself several times over because you'll likely avoid several costly and demoralizing crashes.

When I got into the RC flying hobby, I lost or crashed more than $700 worth of planes during my first two weeks. That's when I buckled down and bought a simulator, and after a couple of weeks' practice, I was a much better pilot, and my crashes were less frequent and less severe. If you're definitely into RC flying for the long term, you can't go wrong buying a simulator.

Don't make the mistake of thinking you can easily learn to fly once you've got a model plane up in the air. Airline pilots receive lots of training on the ground before they venture into the air, and smart RC pilots do the same. Even after you're a proficient pilot, you can continue using your simulator: First, you can use the simulator when outdoor flying is impossible because of the weather. Secondly, you can test-fly new airplane models on the simulator to help you decide which model you'll buy next.

Simulators enable you to take lessons on basic flying skills and aerobatic maneuvers. You can also compete in an online multi-player mode to refine your skills in spot landing, limbo flying, precision bomb dropping, and other activities.

The RC flight simulator field is dominated by three programs: RealFlight, Phoenix R/C Pro, and Aerofly5. All three work on Windows computers (Aerofly is also available for Macs) and cost $100 to $175, depending on the features and whether it includes a transmitter. (You can use your existing transmitter with a flight simulator if it has the proper jack on the back.)

Each of the three leading simulators is quite good, but in my opinion, the graphics on the Phoenix are a bit more realistic. Perhaps the deciding factor is which simulator(s) includes the actual planes you are interested in flying.

Despite all the advantages of having a flight simulator, there's a downside, too. It's possible to develop some bad habits on a simulator and over time, the related "muscle memory" can be awfully hard to un-learn. For example, on a simulator, it's easy to get away with over-controlling the plane, sometimes called a "bank and yank" method, using jerky movements to maneuver the plane. Also, because your depth perception on a simulator is limited, it's hard to practice lining up your plane for a final approach and landing, which is a critical skill.

So it's important to supplement your use of a simulator with some one-on-one flight lessons from friend or colleague. A flesh-and-blood instructor will explain why it's important to make gradual, gentle movements while flying, and it's something you won't get from a simulator. After you've had a couple of lessons, you'll get much more out of your time on the simulator. (The subsequent chapter in this book "Join a Club" will explain how to get free flying lessons at a local flying field.)

Above: Flying the E-flite Apprentice on the Phoenix flight simulator. The experience closely matches flying the real plane at a field—you can choose among "beginner," "intermediate," and "expert" flight modes. Also, you can change the flying location and weather conditions.

Here's a tip for making the Phoenix simulator as realistic as possible. On the top menu, click "View," then "Camera." Then select "Keep ground in view." This provides a more realistic experience of standing at the flying field while viewing your plane in flight.

For more information on the three flight simulators:

Phoenix: http://www.amazon.com/Phoenix-Pro-Simulator-V5-0-DX6i/dp/B00MHVVU7C/

RealFlight: http://www.amazon.com/Great-Planes-Interlink-Flight-Stimulator/dp/B00G7JCWR2/

Aerofly: http://www.aerofly.com/aerofly5/

Battery Charger

Shopping for a battery charger is probably the least exciting part of the RC hobby. But if you're committed to RC flying, a good charger is essential.

If you're on a budget, it's not easy to shell out $50, $100, or even $150 for a charger. But look at it this way: if you're into this hobby, you're going to be investing in new batteries on a regular basis. Charging them with a full-featured charger will keep them in good condition, and the batteries can last three or four years instead of only one year.

Ready-to-fly planes usually come with an inexpensive charger, which never work as well as a full-featured charger. I'm going to recommend three battery chargers that can charge at least a four-cell LiPo battery and cost between $50 and $90. I'm providing the Web address where you can read the full description of these chargers at Amazon.com, along with the customer reviews.

Bastens Easy to use and Fast LiPo Battery Balance Charger:
http://www.amazon.com/dp/B004WPITVQ/
Tenergy TB6-B Balance Charger, Combo Special
http://www.amazon.com/dp/B00466PKE0/
Traxxas 2933 EZ-Peak Plus 6 Amp LiPo and NiMH Charger
http://www.amazon.com/dp/B005FUKQ7M/

The Traxxas charger has a higher capacity (it handles up to six-cell LiPos) but it comes with fewer connection cords than the Bastens models. That's an unfortunate fact of life in the RC plane world—it seems that every plane you buy will come with a different type of battery connector. One innovation that has somewhat solved this problem is the "octopus"-type cord that has a half-dozen or more connections all hanging from the same charging lead, which enables you to connect virtually any type of battery to your charger. Here is an example:

Colossus 19-in-1 Charging Adapters

http://www.amazon.com/dp/B00E001DFC/

One drawback of some battery chargers is that they come with unclear instructions, which can render the device worthless. The devices listed here come with complete, easy-to-understand manuals.

Although I've pointed you in the direction of Amazon.com, there's no particular reason for buying a charger at Amazon, unless you prefer buying from Amazon. Otherwise, your local hobby shop might be an excellent place to shop for chargers, particularly if the sales personnel can demonstrate how to properly charge and balance a LiPo battery. This is one of those cases where a knowledgeable sales staff can be invaluable.

eBay is another online source of RC models and accessories. One shop in particular that provides bargain prices on planes and accessories is Hobb-e-Mart at http://stores.ebay.com/Hobb-e-Mart/ . Their merchandise is often discounted because there is superficial damage to the box or the item is missing one or more components.

Floats

If you have access to a lake or other recreational body of water, you can greatly expand your potential flying area by using floats to convert your aircraft into a seaplane. If you take your plane along on a sailboat trip, you're pretty much guaranteed to have a successful day with at least one of the two activities—if it's too windy to fly, it should be fine sailing weather.

Airplane floats can also be used for landing on snow—a great solution for those winter days when the air temperature is comfortable but the ground is still snow-covered.

Most of the larger plane manufacturers offer floats as inexpensive accessories that switch places with the landing gear. For example, floats for the HobbyZone Super Cub LP cost $24.99, and the set includes a larger propeller to maximize the performance of the Cub on floats. However, taking off and landing on water is trickier than doing it on land. If the plane tips over into the water and the electronics get wet, the damage can be severe.

Above: Taking off from a lake using floats.

If you have trouble finding floats for your plane—or finding them at the right price—you can turn to a specialty manufacturer like SeaPlane Supply of Lake Orion, Michigan. For example, this company sells a kit of 27-inch floats for the E-flite Apprentice for $28, while floats from the original manufacturer cost $49.99. You can see a video of the SeaPlane Supply floats in use here: http://youtu.be/eAOTMEZKDg4 .

SeaPlane Supply sells their floats in a variety of sizes. The floats should range from 75 percent to 80 percent of the length of the fuselage. The shorter the float, the less weight and drag you'll endure while flying, but the tradeoff is you'll lose pitch stability on the water and perhaps flip over with shorter floats. And unfortunately, high-wing trainers are the most likely planes to tip over because the wing is much higher than the water level.

Find SeaPlane Supply at www.seaplanesupply.com.

Cameras

It's hard to believe, but you can buy a one-ounce camcorder and mount it to your wing or fuselage, and re-live your flights as if you were onboard the plane. In particular, I recommend the Mobius Action Camera, which takes high-definition video and costs about $80. See it on

Amazon.com at www.amazon.com/dp/B00DP1WYD2 2/ . This camera is a great example of how the price for small electronics has fallen in recent years while the capabilities have grown. For example, when I bought my first handheld camcorder a dozen years ago, I paid seven times as much money as the Mobius costs. Plus, the old camera weighed about 1.5 pounds—and its picture quality was horrible compared to the Mobius!

To whet your appetite for onboard video, here's a YouTube video of Mobius camera mounted aboard an RC plane: http://youtu.be/-Wfk0rC4PHk .

Another camera popular with RC hobbyists is the GoPro. A version encased in a waterproof housing sells for $199.99 on Amazon at http://www.amazon.com/dp/B00GXKTEUI/ . The GoPro offers state-of-the-art video and audio for a small camera, but it is much larger and heavier than the Mobius, in addition to its higher price.

First Person View (FPV)

First Person View, or FPV, takes onboard video to a whole new level. With a regular camera, you strap it to your plane, fly, and watch the video later. With FPV equipment, however, you watch live video while your plane is still flying. So FPV gives you the sense of actually being onboard the plane while it's in the sky. You're actually piloting the plane with a view from the cockpit—as the live video is fed to a small screen or video goggles.

Until recently, you had to collect the necessary components into a FPV system, which required a lot of research. Today, you can get a ready-to-fly system with a headset for ultra-micro planes for $349.99 from Horizon Hobby. See it at http://bit.ly/1tQkriW .

The inexpensive FPV systems designed for ultra-micro and park-flyer planes have a range of about 150 to 300 feet and require no license to operate. Higher-powered systems are available from vendors like FatShark, and can require a Ham amateur radio license.

For more information about First Person View, view this page: http://www.spektrumrc.com/Technology/FPV.aspx .

Smartphone apps

If you already own a smartphone, it will come in handy during your RC flying. First, it can provide current weather and wind conditions, in addition to forecasts. My favorite app is Weatherbug, which provides current weather and wind conditions, times for sunrise and sunset, forecasting for virtually any neighborhood, plus a radar map. For more detailed information about wind conditions, look for the apps WindAlert and Windfinder—they're both available for iPhone and Android.

Also, you can use the timer function of your phone as a reminder of when it's time to land, which can prevent accidents caused by overtaxing the battery.

Lights for Night Flying

Night flying has become possible recently thanks to the availability of highly efficient LED lights. If you're handy with a soldering iron, you can add strips of LED lights to any of your favorite aircraft. The LEDs can be powered by the flight battery or a separate battery.

Three methods of LED illumination are currently on the market. First, white LED lights are applied to the wingtips and tail, illuminating the plane's surfaces. Second, multi-colored LEDs applied to the surface of the plane radiate light from the plane. Third, LEDs installed inside the foam structure illuminate the plane from within.

If you don't want to install lights yourself, the HobbyKing Flybeam plane comes with lights pre-installed beneath the surface of the plane's foam structure. The photograph below doesn't do it justice; you have to see the Flybeam to appreciate it. I recommend installing an E-flite Apprentice SAFE receiver on the Flybeam (it's part No. EFLR310013, not available from HobbyKing.) With a standard receiver, it's very difficult to slow down this plane for landing. But with the SAFE receiver installed, the Flybeam is a well-mannered trainer aircraft that is also capable of basic aerobatic maneuvers. For more information on installing a SAFE receiver in the Flybeam and other planes, consult this page: http://bit.ly/15NQgjN .

Night flying is lots of fun, but it's best if you practice at dusk for the first few flights. You should restrict your night flying to familiar sites because darkness obscures the ground and obstacles such as trees.

Above: The HobbyKing Flybeam is the first park flyer featuring pre-installed LED lights for night flying. The lighting scheme resembles the traditional navigation lights of full-scale aircraft, with red lights on the left or port side, and green lights on the right or starboard side. Strobe lights on the wingtips help preserve the pilot's orientation when the plane is at high altitudes.

Rolls of LED lights can be purchased at eBay, Amazon, and at some local hobby shops. Three companies specialize in selling pre-built LED systems for a variety of planes:

Aurora RC: www.aurorarc.com/ .

After Dark LED: www.afterdarkled.com .

My Trick RC: http://www.mytrickrc.com/aircraft-products/.

▶ JOIN A CLUB

Lots of people believe it's more fun to fly RC planes when you've got company. You can learn a lot—and make many new friends—by joining a local club. By far the most prominent is the Academy of Model Aeronautics (AMA), which has local chapters across the United States.

The big advantage of joining a local AMA chapter is that many of them operate well-maintained flying fields. For example, in my region of Northern Virginia, the county has set aside a huge section of a park solely for flying model planes. The AMA chapter provides members with access to trainer aircraft and flight instructors, free of charge, both for battery-powered planes and internal-combustion aircraft. After you pass a flight test, you're qualified to fly solo at the club field.

Nothing can match the one-on-one feedback from an experienced teacher. Usually the instructor is equipped with a master transmitter that can take over for the student pilot in case an accident is imminent. In addition to using the club's trainer plane, you can bring your own plane and get assistance with flying it as well.

Another big perk of joining a local club is their aircraft auctions. My club has two auctions each year, one in the fall and one in the spring. These auctions are a gold mine for new pilots looking to acquire planes and accessories. Many of the aircraft auctioned are one-of-a-kind aircraft that were painstakingly built by scratch. And best of all, club auctions tend to be a buyer's market—the winning bids are typically a bargain compared to the original cost of the plane or its replacement value. Club auctions aren't limited to planes; they often include spare parts, batteries, chargers, helicopters, model rockets, and other equipment.

To find the AMA-chartered club closest to you, visit this address: http://www.modelaircraft.org/clubsearch.aspx .

Above: The pit area of the Northern Virginia RC Model Aircraft Club's flying field. The run-up tables, sometimes called "starting benches," are used mainly for internal-combustion planes. The structures secure the plane while the pilot starts the engine.

Above: Browsing auctions items at a local club meeting.

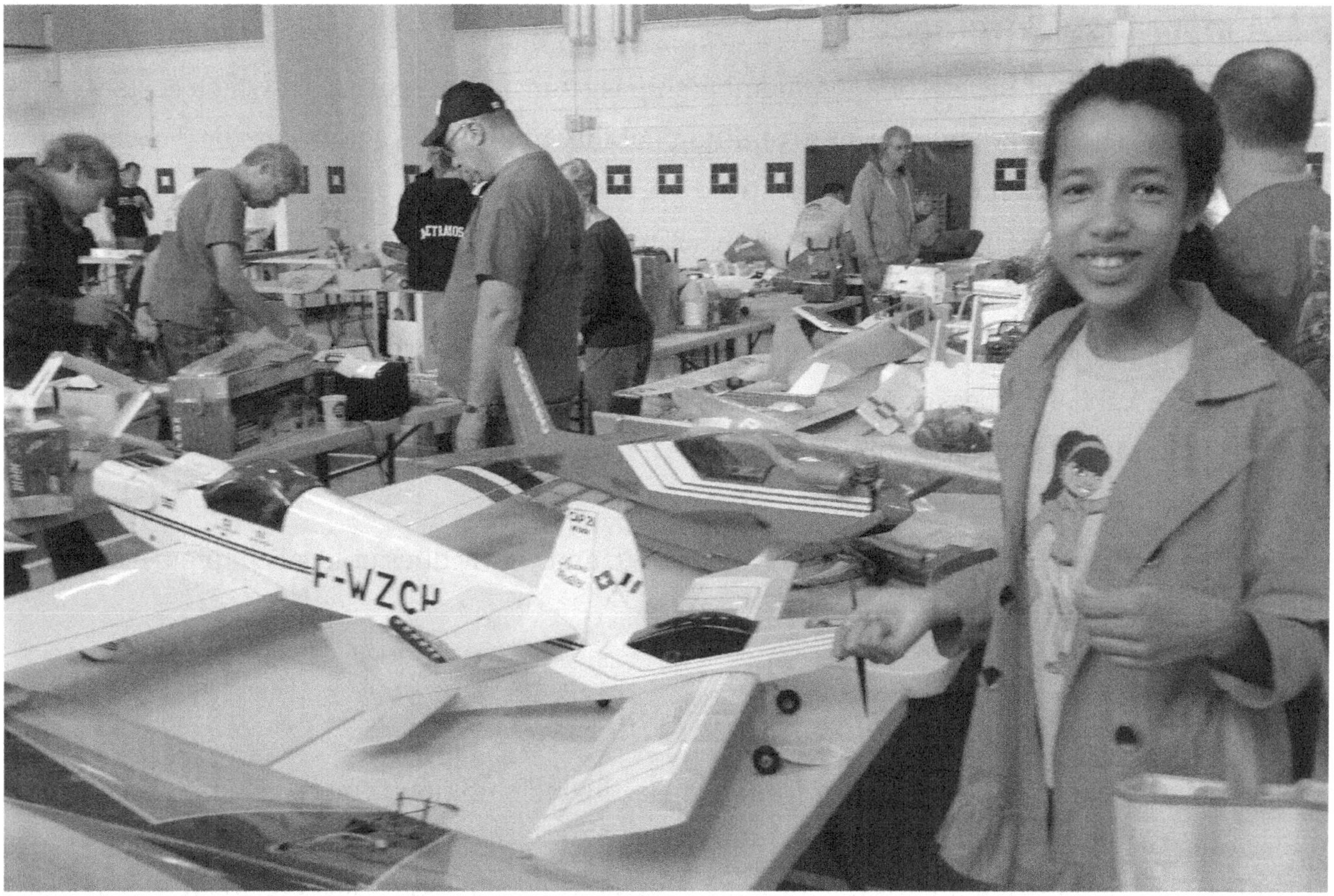

Above: My daughter, Lauren Weber, browsing at an auction.

Above: It's often a buyer's market at club auctions, with some unique planes and accessories being sold for bargain prices.

AMA Insurance Coverage

Another important benefit of AMA membership is its insurance coverage, which costs nothing extra. The policy includes a $2.5 million liability umbrella, $25,000 medical coverage, and $1,000 fire and theft coverage. If you tried purchasing this coverage yourself, it would cost at least $1,000 a year. The AMA covers you wherever you fly, including club fields, parks, and backyards.

The AMA also looks out for your interests in Washington. The group recently worked with Congress to establish a special rule for model aircraft, exempting recreational unmanned aircraft from regulation. AMA membership also includes a monthly magazine featuring how-to articles, product reviews, and an event calendar.

Annual membership in the AMA costs about $60, and yearly dues at local chapters cost about $60 more. It's worth every penny.

Earning the Right to Fly Solo at Your Club Field

To earn the right to fly solo at your local AMA-affiliated club field, you'll have to take at least one lesson, then be recommended by your instructor to take a qualification flight. Although the specific requirements might vary at your local club, here are the kinds of tasks you'll be expected to perform:

- Complete a preflight safety inspection, start your engine, and taxi your plane safely to the runway.
- Demonstrate a satisfactory takeoff and climb out.
- Execute a 180-degree turn away from the flight line and demonstrate control of a straight-line flyby.

Then, on request of the flight instructor, perform:

- A flat horizontal figure-eight in both directions.
- A successful inside loop while maintaining proper altitude and direction.
- Two satisfactory Immelmann turns (also known as a "roll off the top" aerobatic maneuver, in which the plane ascends on a half-loop followed by a half-roll, resulting in level flight in the opposite direction at a higher altitude). Perform one Immelmann turn going away from your location, and one coming toward your location.
- Intentional stall of the aircraft and recovery successfully.

- A successful dead-stick landing: After climbing to an altitude of 200 feet or more, your flight instructor will, without warning, cut the throttle to idle to simulate a dead-stick condition. Your must call out "dead stick" and land your plane on the runway with no throttle.

It takes many hours of practice to perfect these maneuvers. And then it will take nerves of steel to be able to repeat them successfully under the watchful eye of an instructor so that you can qualify to fly solo.

▶ FINDING MORE INFORMATION

We've only scratched the surface of this exciting world of RC flying. Luckily there are hobbyists everywhere eager to share their expertise. You just have to know where to find them. Here are a few locations where you'll find a treasure trove of knowledge, and this is followed by a glossary in the next section to explain specialized terms used in the hobby.

Also, don't hesitate to drop me a line if you have any questions about getting started with RC flying. Email me at steve@weberbooks.com .

RC Groups.com (www.rcgroups.com)

If you search on Google.com for an answer to any technical question you have, such as "what's the best trainer plane?" the top search results will likely be discussions at RC Groups.com. If your question hasn't been covered already, you can register at the site and get answers quickly. RC Groups also has product reviews, videos, and discussions dedicated to aircraft models from every major manufacturer. If you've having an issue with your plane, or are looking for recommendations for a new one, the first place you should visit is RC Groups.com.

Flitetest.com (www.flitetest.com)

Flitetest has an amazing catalog of original videos about everything concerning RC planes—reviews of new models, tutorials on building aircraft, and coverage of airplane events from across North America and the world. If you want to learn more about the hobby, I suggest that you subscribe to Flitetest's YouTube channel and check the website regularly. The enthusiasm of the folks at Flitetest is contagious, and their videos, podcasts, and articles provide a never-ending stream of entertainment and valuable expertise.

You can view the Flitetest podcasts at iTunes here: http://bit.ly/1r5AhkW .

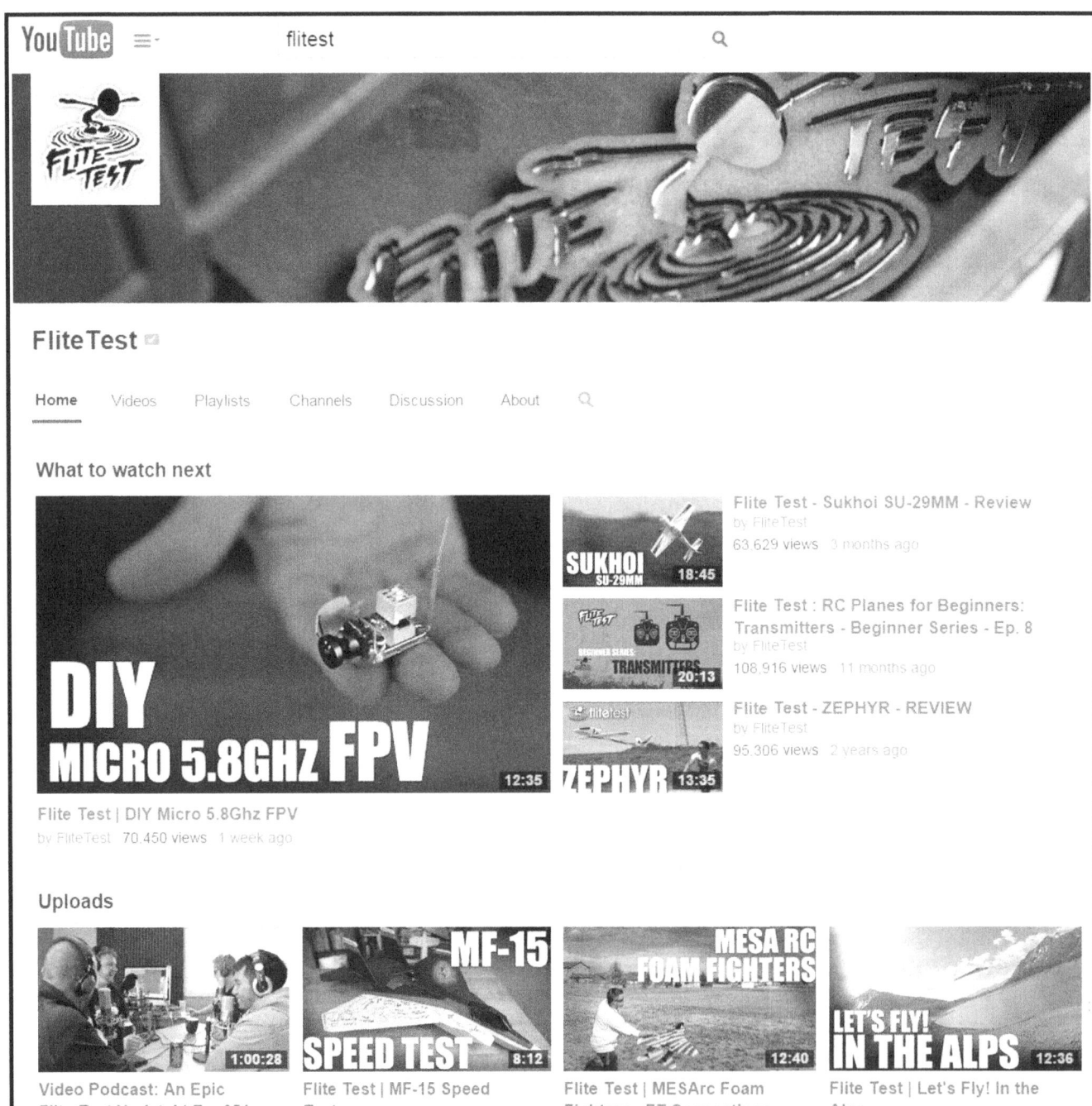

Above: The YouTube channel for Flitetest.

More RC plane reviews

Two more great sources of video reviews of RC planes:

ChuckTSeeker: **http://bit.ly/1vwGihi** .

Around Tuit RC: **http://bit.ly/1HvH5CX** .

Flight Instruction

The Academy of Model Aeronautics maintains a list of independent flight instructors at this address: http://www.modelaircraft.org/programs/rcfi.aspx .

Recommended Reading

These books are available for order through Amazon.com, your local bookstore, and in some cases, your public library.

One Week to Solo by David Scott. The central solo techniques that all good flyers use are brought to the forefront and systematically assembled to enable beginning RC pilots to achieve Solo in the shortest amount of time.

Park Flying 1-2-3D by David Scott. Concise lessons and hundreds of illustrations with matching control stick diagrams. Helps pilots bypass common mistakes and enhance practice effectiveness by focusing attention on controlling what the airplane does instead of merely reacting to it.

▶ GLOSSARY

3-D Expert aerobatic flying, such as hovering, rolls, spins and loops, practiced by experienced pilots.

Aileron A hinged flight control surface usually attached to the trailing edge of each wing; controls the aircraft's roll or bank.

AS3X technology A stabilization system made by E-flite, which smoothes out turbulence of gusty wind conditions. AS3X can make a small plane handle like a much larger plane by making it more steady in flight.

Attitude The angle of the plane in relation to the horizon.

Barrel roll A corkscrew maneuver in which an aircraft completes a spiral turn on its longitudinal axis.

Binding The process of pairing a plane's receiver with your handheld transmitter. The process is begun by placing a "binding plug" in your receiver.

Bind-n-fly This usually means that an airplane is being sold without the transmitter, and that you can bind the receiver with a transmitter you already own. This is a trademarked term by Horizon Hobby.

Brushless motor The current standard for electric RC plane motors; more efficient and powerful than the predecessor "brushed" motors.

Buddy box RC flying instructors connect their transmitter with a student's transmitter so that the instructor can take control of the plane in the event of a problem.

Center of gravity (CG or CoG) The point over which the aircraft would balance. The RC pilot can vary the CG by moving the flight batter forward or aft in its compartment, among other things.

Clevis A U-shaped fastening device with two holes at the end for a pin to pass through. Connects your servo arm with the control surface.

Control horn A device that helps deflect a control surface. Servo push rods are connected to the control horn.

Control surface A movable surface that influences the direction of flight, such as a rudder, elevator or aileron.

Crosswind Wind blowing across the angle being flown. This is a challenge for pilots, who should take off and land into the wind when possible.

Deadstick landing When a pilot loses motor power and is forced to land.

Drag Sometimes called "wind resistance," the aerodynamic force impeding a plane's movement through the air.

DSM2 The current technological standard for RC plane transmitters; resists interference and latency.

Dual rates A switch on the transmitter that can select different throw rates for controls; increases the maneuverability of a plane.

Elevator The horizontal control surface on the tail that pitches the plane up or down.

ESC The electronic speed controller used to vary an electric motor's speed.

Fin Another word for the "vertical stabilizer."

Flap A hinged surface mounted on the training edge of wings; assists with landing by enabling the pilot to reduce airspeed without causing the plane to stall.

Flare During the last part of a landing, using the elevator to pitch the plane's nose up slightly. This bleeds off speed and makes for a softer landing.

Fuselage The main body of an aircraft.

Hand launch An alternative to taking off by rolling along the landing strip. The pilot or an assistant tosses the plane forward as throttle is applied.

Horizontal stabilizer The horizontal surface at the rear of the plane where the elevator is attached.

Lift The upward pressure created by a wing's movement through the air.

Loop An aerobatic maneuver in which the plane completes a vertical circle.

Low-Voltage Cutoff (LVC) A circuit that restricts power to the motor when the flight battery is discharged to a certain point; requires an immediate landing.

Mode 2 The standard transmitter system in which the left stick controls throttle and rudder, and the right stick controls elevator and ailerons.

Park flyer Small planes that can be flown within a large park or athletic field; sometimes called a "slow flyer."

Pitch An aircraft's rotation around the side-to-side axis; controlled by elevators.

Plug-n-play Ready-to-fly aircraft sold without the receiver.

Range check A preflight procedure where the pilot walks about 100 feet from the aircraft and verifies that the plane's control surfaces move correctly in response to inputs from the transmitter.

RC The abbreviation for "radio controlled" aircraft. Some hobbyists also use the abbreviation to refer to "remote control."

Receiver A component in the plane that receives signals from the transmitter and interprets control instructions from the pilot.

Roll An aircraft's rotation around the front-to-back axis; controlled by ailerons.

RTF Abbreviation for "ready to fly," when an RC aircraft is sold with everything required for flight, including transmitter, batteries, and receiver.

Rudder The control surface on the trailing edge of a plane's vertical stabilizer; controls yaw.

Rx Abbreviation for receiver.

SAFE Technology Abbreviation for sensor assisted flight envelope, which offers multiple flight modes, such as beginner, intermediate and advanced, in which the pilot is prevented from extreme movements that could cause a crash.

Scale An RC plane that is a miniature model of a real full-sized aircraft.

Servo. An electronic device inside the plane that translates the pilot's transmitter instructions for moving control surfaces on the aircraft.

Spin A type of stall resulting in rotation around the vertical axis and causing a downward rotating path.

Stall A rapid decrease in lift by having the nose too high or the airspeed too low.

Transmitter A handheld device containing the control sticks and other switches to control the airplane; sometimes called a "radio."

Trimming Small adjustments made to control surfaces via the transmitter to enable straight and level flight.

Tx Abbreviation for transmitter.

Yaw An aircraft's rotation around the vertical axis; controlled by rudder.

Vertical stabilizer The fin on the aft end of the fuselage that provides directional stability.

Index

Academy of Model Aeronautics, 51
Aerofly flight simulator, 45
After Dark LED, 50
ailerons, 10, 61
airfoil, 11
almost ready to fly, 12
AMA, 51
Amazon.com, 46
Apprentice, 21
Apprentice SAFE receiver, 49
Around Tuit RC, 58
AS3X technology, 61
attitude, 61
Aurora RC, 50
barrel roll, 61
battery charger, 45
binding, 61
bind-n-fly, 12, 61
brushless motor, 61
buddy box, 61
camcorder, 47
cameras, 47
center of gravity, 61
CG, 61
Champ, 13
charging adapters, 46
ChuckTSeeker, 58
clevise, 61
CoG, 61
control direction test, 32
control horn, 61
control surface, 62
crosswind, 62
deadstick landing, 62

Delta Ray, 19
DHC-2 Beaver, 29
dihedral, 11
down elevator, 33
drag, 9, 62
DSM2, 62
dual rates, 62
Du-Bro Electric Flyer Hinge Tape, 42
Duet, 14
eBay, 46
electronic speed controller, 62
elevator, 10, 62
ESC, 62
FatShark, 48
fin, 62
First Person View, 48
flap, 62
flare, 62
flaring, 37
flight simulator, 43
Flitetest, 57
floats, 46
flutter, 41
Flybeam, 49
flying solo, 54
Foam Tac, 42
FPV, 48
fuselage, 10, 62
GoPro camera, 48
Gorilla Glue, 42
gravity, 9
Great Planes ElectriFly EP Super Sportster, 28
hand launch, 62
hand launching, 40

high wing, 11
Hobb-e-Mart, 46
HobbyKing Flybeam, 49
HobbyZone Champ, 13
HobbyZone Duet, 14
HobbyZone Sport Cub S, 16
horizontal stabilizer, 62
Immelmann turns, 54
insurance, 54
landing, 36
LED lights, 49
lift, 62
Lift, 9
loop, 62
low-voltage cutoff, 38
Mobius Action Camera, 47
Mode 2, 62
My Trick RC, 50
neck strap, 40
night flying, 49
oval pattern, 33
overcorrecting, 34
packing tape, 42
park flyer, 62
Parkzone Radian, 23
Parkzone Sport Cub, 25
ParkZone T-28 Trojan, 26
Phoenix flight simulator, 45
pitch, 62
plug-n-play, 12, 63
Professional Welder Adhesive, 42
propeller pulses, 41
R/C, 63
Radian, 17, 23
range check, 32, 63

RC Groups.com, 57
ready-to-fly, 12
RealFlight flight simulator, 45
receiver, 63
roll, 63
RTF, 63
rudder, 9, 63
SAFE receiver, 49
SAFE technology, 12, 36
SAFE Technology, 63
scale, 63
SeaPlane Supply, 47
Sensor-Assisted Flight Envelope, 12
servo, 63
spin, 63
Sport Cub S, 16
stall, 63
Super Sportster, 28
T-28 Trojan, 26
taking off, 32
tape, 42
thrust, 9
transmitter, 10
trim, 38, 63
troubleshooting, 41
Tx, 63
UMX Radian, 17
up elevator, 33
vertical stabilizer, 10, 63
video recorders, 47
Weatherbug, 48
WindAlert, 49
Windfinder, 49
yaw, 63

Made in the USA
Monee, IL
12 October 2020